reimagining
the public intellectual
in education

Studies in the
Postmodern Theory of Education

Shirley R. Steinberg
General Editor

Vol. 463

The Counterpoints series is part of the Peter Lang Education list.
Every volume is peer reviewed and meets
the highest quality standards for content and production.

PETER LANG
New York • Bern • Frankfurt • Berlin
Brussels • Vienna • Oxford • Warsaw

reimagining
the public intellectual
in education

making scholarship matter

edited by CYNTHIA GERSTL-PEPIN
and CYNTHIA REYES

PETER LANG
New York • Bern • Frankfurt • Berlin
Brussels • Vienna • Oxford • Warsaw

Library of Congress Cataloging-in-Publication Data

Reimagining the public intellectual in education: making scholarship matter /
Edited by Cynthia Gerstl-Pepin, Cynthia Reyes.
pages cm. — (Counterpoints: Studies in the Postmodern Theory of Education ; Vol. 463)
Includes bibliographical references and index.
1. Educational leadership—Social aspects. 2. Intellectuals—Social conditions.
3. Critical pedagogy. 4. Education and globalization. 5. Postmodernism and education.
I. Gerstl-Pepin, Cynthia, editor. II. Reyes, Cynthia, editor.
LC89.R45   371.2—dc23   2014024856
ISBN 978-1-4331-2521-8 (hardcover)
ISBN 978-1-4331-2520-1 (paperback)
ISBN 978-1-4539-1426-7 (e-book)
ISSN 1058-1634

Bibliographic information published by **Die Deutsche Nationalbibliothek**.
Die Deutsche Nationalbibliothek lists this publication in the "Deutsche
Nationalbibliografie"; detailed bibliographic data are available
on the Internet at http://dnb.d-nb.de/.

The paper in this book meets the guidelines for permanence and durability
of the Committee on Production Guidelines for Book Longevity
of the Council of Library Resources.

Printed in the United States of America

To the leaders, teachers, communities, families, students, and researchers
working to improve schools
and
To Cynthia Gerstl-Pepin's sons, Reid and Ethan, and her husband, Craig
and
To Cynthia Reyes' children, Elliot and Monica, and her husband, Brian.

You inspire us every day to make a difference for children everywhere.

Contents

Preface

A Case for Emphasizing the "Public" in Public Intellectual

CYNTHIA GERSTL-PEPIN AND CYNTHIA REYES

INTRODUCTION

Dr. David Parenti (academic): We get the grant, we study the problem, we propose solutions. If they listen, they listen. If they don't, it still makes for great research. What we publish on this is gonna get a lot of attention.

Howard "Bunny" Colvin (former police officer): From who?

Dr. David Parenti: From other researchers, academics.

Howard "Bunny" Colvin: Academics?! What, they gonn' study your study? [chuckles and shakes head] When do this shit change?

—*The Wire*, Season 4, Final Grades Episode (Simon & Johnson, 2006)
© [2006], Home Box Office, Inc. All Rights Reserved, used with permission

The excerpt above from the television show *The Wire* laments the shutting down of a successful educational program that was helping troubled middle school students. This excerpt is emblematic of the startling lack of connection between academic research and meaningful policy solutions. In academia, academic publication is privileged over community needs. It is this disconnect that the character Bunny Colvin laments and that we seek to explore in this book. While it is the "intellectual" side of the term "public intellectual" that academics have tended to focus on in debates and scholarship, we believe that it is the public side of the equation that needs more focus and attention from education scholars.

In a world where research must be presented as objective if it is to make an impact on policymaking, there exists a tension between the notions of an academic researcher as a neutral professional and as a policy advocate. Nowhere in the public discussion is it stated that all research is socially constructed, whether it involves naturalistic inquiry or experimental design. Despite the best attempts of the researcher to use objective forms of research such as quantitative methods, including quasi-experimental design, the very research questions we ask are difficult to disentangle from our value systems, training, beliefs, and historical context from which a researcher emerges (Gunzenhauser & Gerstl-Pepin, 2006). While naturalistic inquiry and qualitative forms of inquiry often acknowledge bias, much quantitative research is wrapped in seemingly objective methodologies that claim to control for research bias.

Yet one need only look historically at objective research studies such as the Tuskegee syphilis experiment conducted between 1932 and 1972 (Jones, 1993) or the Nazi "scientific" experiments (Baumslag, 2005) to see how objective methodologies can be shaped by culturally biased researchers. Nazi researchers subscribing to the Nazi ideology of the superiority of the Aryan race conducted numerous inhumane experiments on concentration camp victims who were considered racially inferior. White researchers in the Tuskegee experiment discovered a treatment for syphilis in 1940 but neglected to inform the African American sharecroppers in the study that there was an effective treatment, thus allowing them to suffer and in some cases die from the disease. These studies show that researchers are human after all and not beyond reproach even when utilizing objective research designs. So when qualitative forms of research are presented and acknowledge the bias of the researcher, they can be easily dismissed. Yet the irony is that quantitative approaches can often be shaped by bias but presented as objective.

Media coverage of educational issues is rife with self-appointed experts on education (with little or no research training in education) such as Steven Brill (founder of CourtTV and *American Lawyer* magazine) or Joel Klein (former New York City schools chancellor whose professional training is in health and constitutional law) who have claimed space in public discussions to define educational problems and solutions. These public speakers dominate public dialogues on education, going so far as to write magazine articles for *The Atlantic, The Wall Street Journal,* and the *New Yorker* and, in Steven Brill's case, a book targeted to the public, *Class Warfare: Inside the Fight to Fix America's Schools* (2012). A variety of self-appointed experts promote solutions to continuing national debates on such polarizing issues as national testing, charter schools and school choice, or higher education costs. In many cases they present data and information as if their opinions are based on objective truths.

At a local level in our own rural northeast state, we witness ongoing public debates on environmental and educational issues, such as the role of wind and solar energy, the nuclear power plant, and racism in one school district in a predominantly White state. We continue to hear a meager response from academic voices at the local university, even as these local issues have critical relevance to the larger national discussion on the economy and the immigration debate in Arizona. There may be isolated conversations, but there is a noticeable absence of more intentional university voices engaging in these debates in the public arena. Molnar (2006) argues that very few scholars are interested in joining in public debate, and many more are too consumed with the "promotion regime" to become interested in joining discussions (p. 64). There may even be fear of retaliation for speaking out on school issues, especially when their programs depend heavily on local schools for pre-service teacher clinical internships. Such relationships are vital for a strong teacher education program. Academics, particularly in education, walk a fine line of partnering with local schools yet bringing into the classroom current local issues, even if the latter are polarizing and foster controversial debate. But where are the researchers in these academic dialogues at all levels? This book seeks to address this issue by sharing the stories of scholars who are seeking to engage in public dialogue and reclaim space for reasoned dialogue on education.

WHEN "INTELLECTUAL" DEBATES TRUMP PUBLIC CONCERNS

The notion of the public intellectual has many historical connotations and has been written about in broad terms across disciplines (Jacoby, 2000; Posner, 2002; Said, 1994). But what constitutes the "public" in public intellectual? It has been a term that has been used to describe scholars who seek to share their research with the public. Little work has been done, however, to examine the role of a public intellectual in the field of education (Cochran-Smith, 2006a, 2006b). Authors such as Cochran-Smith (2006a) see how the public dialogue on education has evolved over the years and highlight the critical need for public intellectuals (scholars) in the field of education. Given that state and federal policies govern much of education, it is critical that the public and policymakers reclaim the public dialogue on education so that it can be opened up to include scholars who are informed and knowledgeable about educational problems. Cochran-Smith (2006b) defines the role of the public intellectual in education as requiring that "in whatever public realm one has influence and access, one is obliged to offer critique of policies and practices he or she sees as problematic in terms of logic or evidence or that will not serve the best interests of schoolchildren and teachers" (p. 97).

Few university-based scholars have sought to enter public debates, and when they have, it is often challenging to move away from traditional academic discourse. For example, Ladson-Billings and Tate (2006) offer a collection of essays from scholars who write compellingly on the intersections of race, poverty, power, and education. The editors use Hurricane Katrina as a backdrop for discussing the politics of neoliberalism, the privatization of education, and accountability and the economic market. The arguments are empirically supported, and the scholarly prowess of each of the authors is reflected and legitimized in the discourse and passion they use to describe their topics. Yet the audience for whom this book is intended is other scholars who are interested in informing public conversations, debates, and policy formation around education. The language and discourse of the book is academic and abstract; however, some authors express anger and frustration with education policy decisions driven by political agendas rather than the best interests of students and schools. The anger and frustration is often the result of inhumane educational reform and policies. Ironically, the very public that is most affected by these dangerous policies—the ones most marginalized and disenfranchised in the school system—do not have access to these types of academic texts and research.

Even if such texts are neither appropriate to nor meant for the general public, how might the very crucial and compelling topics that affect the very individuals who need to make the decisions or who need to choose among the educational policies be made more fluid and translatable? How can those individuals become better informed? Which texts do they read? Furthermore, how might the more academic text by Ladson-Billings and Tate (2006) and other academic tomes inspire, encourage, and move education scholars to make research more accessible to the general public? For the purposes of this book, we choose to build upon the notion of a public intellectual but seek to do so in a way that makes the term more accessible. Specifically, we choose to use the term public *scholar* as opposed to public intellectual to refer to scholars who seek to share their research outside of academia.

The general problem with being a public scholar in the university is the lack of an institutional reward system that encourages scholars to make their work more accessible to the public. Assistant professors must secure tenure, and even associate professors, upon receiving tenure, are kept busy with teaching, advising, and service to the university community. The system provides neither incentive nor inspiration for creatively imagining such a goal. According to Molnar (2006),

> a public intellectual in a university setting must inevitably hover uncomfortably between being an outsider with academically sound ideas that challenge the received wisdom of policy and practice and being someone who maintains durable long-term relationships with the policymaking world beyond the boundaries of the academy. (p. 65)

This dual role can present many challenges, since most higher education institutions reinforce reward systems that favor academic work over community engagement.

USING STORIES TO MAKE WRITING MORE ACCESSIBLE

Rather than engage in another academic exercise in which scholars write about the notion of the public intellectual in abstract terms, we have gathered together the stories of academics who are engaged in public debates. Clandinin and Connelly (2000) see narrative experience (personal stories) as an important facet of understanding educational life, and given this book's goal of reclaiming the public dialogue in education, we have chosen narrative storytelling as a means for creating this understanding. By having a diverse set of authors personally tell their stories and share their experiences as public scholars, we seek to show the various ways in which educational researchers can make their work more accessible to the general public (including those most affected by educational policy decisions such as teachers, parents, students, and community members). The diverse (in terms of culture, gender, academic or not, and politics) public scholars highlighted in the book acknowledge that the policymaking arena is rife with value conflicts that can lead to dismissing or ignoring research if it does not fit with political agendas (Dery, 1990). The focus of the chapters is on lessons learned by public scholars engaging in multiple public arenas from the local to the national and international—from classrooms, school board meetings, blogs, newspaper editorials, media outlets, international programs, cyberspace, Web 2.0, and so on.

ORGANIZATION OF THE BOOK

This preface situates the book within current challenges facing educational researchers as they attempt to inform public debates. To emphasize the "public" in public intellectual, the book is structured around three themes. The first theme examines the potential for making academic language accessible. The second theme examines how scholars can engage in public debates through the news media and Web 2.0 outlets. Finally, the third theme examines the personal dilemmas faced by scholars who engage in this type of work. The book concludes with a final chapter that highlights suggestions emerging from each chapter as to how educational researchers can work to share their research and scholarship in public arenas. The following provides an outline of each of the sections and chapters in the book.

SECTION ONE: MAKING ACADEMIC LANGUAGE ACCESSIBLE

In this section, the authors consider how language can play a role in how a public intellectual shapes her writing for a public audience. Writers in this section aim to highlight their personal struggles with using language to describe the experiences of the individuals who inhabit schools: children, teachers, parents, and staff. They share the difficulties in writing compelling stories about individuals working and learning in schools in order to shed light on the many challenges facing education in light of shifting demographics, inequities, technologies, politics, and economics. Yet personal stories of this kind are generally overshadowed by publicized reporting of standardized reading and writing scores that too often paint a picture of failure within the schools. Without the personal stories of children and teachers at work, the authors fear that the public rarely witnesses the human side of schooling.

The authors in this section explore the ways they use language to write personally about education, particularly children and teachers, in order to lend a personal face to the reported test scores the public receives. Chapter 1, "Crisscrossing from Classrooms to Cartoons: Social Science Satire," by Michael Giangreco, provides an insightful example of how the medium of cartoons can be used as a way to translate academic research and language into a format that is easily understood in public arenas and can have broad appeal via the Internet. In Chapter 2, "'Languaging Their Lives,' Places of Engagement, and Collaborations with Urban Youth," Valerie Kinloch discusses how she simultaneously provides space in her research for the youth she studies who she views as public scholars (intellectuals) and how they inform how she works in their communities as well as how she shares her research in public arenas. In Chapter 3, "Reframing: We Are Not Public Intellectuals; We are Movement Intellectuals," Margarita Machado-Casas, Belinda Flores, and Enrique Murillo, Jr., suggest that the term public intellectual is subtractive and suggest instead that, for their own work, the term Movement Intellectuals is more appropriate, given their call to action and grassroots efforts to redefine research and provide space for the perspectives of cultural groups that have traditionally been marginalized in research as well as public discussions. In Chapter 4, "Scholarly Personal Narrative as a Way to Connect the Academy to the World," Robert Nash explores how narrative writing and storytelling provide one way of making academic language accessible to public debates.

SECTION TWO: ENGAGING THE PUBLIC THROUGH MEDIA AND WEB 2.0

This section acknowledges the rise of the electronic information age, which is constantly shifting and changing. The authors will address the benefits and challenges of using twenty-first-century media outlets to disseminate their research. In Chapter 5, "When a Public Intellectual Speaks Out But No One Hears Her, Does She Exist?" Susan Ohanian examines her own journey in exposing how media outlets can marginalize academics in favor of more mainstream political players. In Chapter 6, "The Naked Seminar: Blogging as Public Education Outside the Classroom," Sherman Dorn explores how he developed his own blog to inform the public on pressing educational debates. In Chapter 7, "The Public Intellectual: The Changing Context; Implications for Attributes and Practices," William Mathis examines the shifting role of educational researchers over the years and the rise of corporate media outlets, shares his personal experiences of engaging in educational policy debates and news media coverage, and identifies the personal attributes required these days to work in the contentious field of education policy. He also provides strategies and practices that can be utilized by educational researchers to enter public debates.

SECTION THREE: PERSONAL DILEMMAS

What are the particular dilemmas confronting the work of the public scholar? What constitutes the reporting of ethics, quality, or authority in both realms? In this section, authors examine the challenge of writing to the general public and writing for their profession. In Chapter 8, "Reflections of a 'Stunt Intellectual': Caught in the Crosshairs of 'Public' Controversy," William Ayers explores his very public engagement in the public media arena. In Chapter 9, "Traveling Down a Desire Line: Surviving Where Academia and Community Meet," JuliAnna Ávila shares her struggles with her role as a public scholar and the challenges of balancing the requirements of working in academia with the very real needs of the communities in which she has worked, such as post-Katrina New Orleans. In Chapter 10, "Conversations That Matter: Community-Based Practice in Support of the Public Good," Alan and Barri Tinkler share their community-based engagement in their local community and argue that this type of work is critical to community improvement and breaking down boundaries between academic goals and community needs. In Chapter 11, "An Inevitable Dichotomy...*Really?* Harmonizing Public Intellectual Work *with* Academic Work," Steven Jay Gross articulates his struggles in balancing his academic research and writing with his desire to influence unjust and harmful policies and his efforts at engaging other academics in efforts for strategic change.

SECTION FOUR: IMPLICATIONS

In Chapter 12, "Reimagining the Public Intellectual in Education: Making Scholarship Matter," we (Reyes & Gerstl-Pepin) examine the implications of the stories of public scholars captured in the book and suggest multiple ways in which education scholars can play a role in contributing to public debates from the local level to the national and international levels.

The authors' insights in this collective of experiences illuminate how education data is transformed and translated in a meaningful way to the general public. The chapters capture multiple, personal stories of researchers engaged in exploring what it means to be a public scholar.

REFERENCES

Baumslag, N. (2005). *Murderous medicine: Nazi doctors, human experimentation, and typhus.* Westport, CT: Praeger.

Brill, S. (2012). *Class warfare: Inside the fight to fix America's schools.* New York: Simon & Schuster.

Clandinin, D. J., & Connelly, F. M. (2000). *Narrative inquiry: Experience and story in qualitative research.* San Francisco: Jossey-Bass.

Cochran-Smith, M. (2006a). Teacher education and the need for public intellectuals. *New Educator, 2*(3), 1547–1688.

Cochran-Smith, M. (2006b). Thirty editorials later: Signing off as editor. *Journal of Teacher Education, 57*(2), 95–101.

Dery, D. (1990). *Data and policy change: The fragility of data in the policy context.* Suffolk, England: Kluwer Academic Publishers.

Gunzenhauser, M.G., & Gerstl-Pepin, C.I. (2006). Engaging graduate education: A pedagogy for epistemological and theoretical diversity. *Review of Higher Education, 29*(3), 319–346.

Jacoby, R. (2000). *The last intellectuals: American culture in the age of academe.* New York: Basic Books.

Jones, J.H. (1993). *Bad blood: The Tuskegee syphilis experiment.* New York: Free Press.

Ladson-Billings, G., & Tate, W.F. (Eds.). (2006). *Education research in the public interest: Social justice, action, and policy.* New York: Teachers College Press.

Molnar, A. (2006). Public intellectuals and the university. In G. Ladson-Billings & W. Tate (Eds.), *Education research in the public interest: Social justice, action, and policy.* New York: Teachers College Press.

Posner, R.A. (2002). *Public intellectuals: A study of decline.* Cambridge, MA: Harvard University Press.

Said, E. (1994). *Representations of the intellectual: The 1993 Reith lectures.* New York: Vintage Press.

Simon, D. (Writer), & Johnson, C. (Director). (2006). Final grades [Television series episode]. In D. Simon & E. Burns (Executive producers), *The wire.* New York: HBO Time Warner.

Making Academic Language Accessible

CHAPTER ONE

Crisscrossing from Classrooms to Cartoons

Social Science Satire

MICHAEL F. GIANGRECO

INTRODUCTION

Within my chosen field—special education—I am known to a substantial set of individuals (many of whom become flustered at the mere prospect of attempting to correctly spell or pronounce my last name) simply as *the cartoon guy*. I have accepted and even come to embrace this somewhat anonymous moniker, recognizing that my influence on public discourse is now inextricably linked to my work creating a collection of satirical cartoons that lampoon the absurdities and realities of special education (Giangreco, 1998, 1999, 2000, 2002, 2007). Despite a traditional academic scholarship record that includes a line of empirical research about inclusive education for students with disabilities and nearly 200 publications (e.g., peer-reviewed journal articles, books, and book chapters) dating back to 1982, it has been the translation of research findings and related issues about special education into cartoons that has struck a chord in the field among professionals from a variety of education and allied health disciplines, families who have children with disabilities, and policymakers.

Cartoons can serve as an effective, albeit unconventional, vehicle to extend the reach of conventionally published research findings to a broader audience in ways people seem to enjoy and remember. In this chapter I describe (a) the early experiences that positioned me to satirize my own field, (b) the reasons I extended my work from traditional scholarship genres to include satirical cartoons, (c) the creative process, (d) the challenges associated with disseminating satirical work, and (e) the impact of cartoons on shaping dialogue and encouraging positive changes in attitudes and practices. Cartooning has not replaced my interest in pursuing conventional research and academic publication as valued outlets for sharing data and ideas. Quite the contrary; cartoons have functioned synergistically to spur new insights, research questions, and scholarship by helping to elucidate the continuing challenges faced by students with disabilities, their families, and service providers.

EARLY INFLUENCES: BECOMING AN INADVERTENT SCHOLAR

I consider myself an inadvertent scholar. I did not set out to conduct research, write for publication, or travel nationally and internationally to lend my voice to the public dialogue on special education in an effort to influence hearts, minds, and practices. Instead my scholarship role developed organically over time. My initial aim simply was to be a special education teacher and to be of service to students with developmental, intellectual, and multiple disabilities and their families by working directly with them and in collaboration with colleagues in related fields (e.g., speech-language pathologists, occupational therapists, physical therapists, and school psychologists). Even though my early career years of direct service are now in the rearview mirror, I still think of myself first and foremost as a special education teacher. To this day I am reluctant to accept the label "scholar" or "public intellectual." I have a sneaking suspicion that such designations may be just as likely to create distance between me and the primary audiences I seek to engage (i.e., teachers, special educators, school administrators, and families who have children with disabilities) than to open the doors to dialogue and progress.

I feel especially fortunate that my first two jobs in the disability field (which I held prior to becoming a special education teacher) involved living in community with people who had disabilities. For over 2 years prior to teaching, I worked as a residential counselor in a group home for adults with developmental disabilities, some of whom were being transitioned out of state-run institutions. (It was the 1970s and the deinstitutionalization movement was in high gear.) Our jobs were to help people live their lives. We prepared and ate meals together, went shopping and elsewhere in the community, managed a household, and spent time getting to know each other as people. This residence was their home, not a "treatment facility," so every effort was made to create a homelike setting, to the extent that this can exist when several strangers are thrown together in a living space. A range of more contemporary community living options exist today, but advancement has not kept up with demand.

While the group home experience was formative, the second early experience was even more influential in setting the foundation for my future work and, eventually, my efforts at cartooning. It is only in retrospect that I can now connect these dots. For seven summers during college and my early teaching years, I worked as a camp counselor at a place called Cradle Beach along the shore of Lake Erie. There, children with the full range of disabilities and children without disabilities from economically disadvantaged, inner-city Buffalo neighborhoods attended camp together. Every camper could participate in any and every activity the camp had to offer, regardless of his or her physical, sensory, intellectual, or social/behavioral characteristics. The emphasis was on playing together, having fun together, and applying our collective creative abilities to explore the boundaries of possibility.

Being responsible for children 24/7, providing personal care supports (e.g., feeding, dressing, toileting, mobility) for those with disabilities who needed it, helping to resolve conflicts between children, and consoling a camper in the middle of the night who was awakened by a nightmare were some of the experiences that provided a tiny glimpse into the responsibilities parents routinely assumed for their children with special needs. Nothing at camp was "special," and everything was special because all of it was ordinary, no matter who was doing it or what supports needed to be put in place for it to happen. Camp had arts and crafts, not art therapy; sing-alongs, not music therapy; a nature hut, not pet therapy; swimming every day (including an optional Polar Bear swim before breakfast and night swims under the lights), not hydrotherapy; sports and games, not gross motor training. In this environment, where differences of many stripes (e.g., ability, race, or socioeconomic status) were all accepted as "normal," expected and unlikely friendships were formed—no need for social skills training. I do not recall terms like "integration" or "inclusion" being used during my years at camp; generally, they were moot because everyone was included. Without realizing it at the time, this experience established the foundation that blossomed into my career-long advocacy for inclusive education.

I credit these two early experiences with inoculating me, at least to some extent, from professional socialization in the "helping professions" that, maybe inadvertently, encourages some service providers to think about people with disabilities primarily as clients or students, rather than simply as people first. These formative experiences helped me recognize the power and possibilities of inclusive environments and opportunities. Later it allowed me to recognize some of the absurdities that my field proffered as standard professional practices and gave me the impetus to openly challenge them and the desire to pursue better alternatives.

What I did not realize at the outset of my career, but which quickly became apparent once my work began as a special educator, was just how dysfunctional—albeit well intended—my chosen profession was and continues to be on certain levels. Discrimination against people with disabilities continues to be cloaked in the guise of benevolence, and too many pieces of the teaching, learning, and service delivery puzzle in schools do not logically fit together. While blatant examples of discrimination still exist, today we must be vigilant in recognizing and exposing more subtle and insidious micro-exclusions. For example, researchers observed a relatively common and problematic phenomenon whereby students with disabilities are physically placed in regular classrooms, only to be isolated *within* the classroom (Giangreco, Edelman, Luiselli, & MacFarland, 1997) (see Figure 1.1). My roles in public education as a special education teacher, school administrator, and university professor have led me to be an unapologetic advocate for extending inclusive educational opportunities for students with the full range of disabilities in general education classes and for appropriately supported access to the same range of opportunities as their peers without disabilities. As it turns out, cartoons can be effective vehicles to advance a progressive agenda of change.

ISLAND IN THE MAINSTREAM
MRS. JONES AND MRS. COOPER ARE STILL TRYING TO FIGURE OUT WHY FRED DOESN'T FEEL LIKE PART OF THE CLASS.

Figure 1.1. Island in the Mainstream.

EXTENDING FROM THE TRADITIONAL TO THE SATIRICAL

Under the tutelage of talented and productive scholars at the three universities from which I earned graduate degrees (the University of Vermont, the University of Virginia, and Syracuse University), the faculty continually reminded us of our responsibility to document and publicly share our work. It was not enough to merely attempt or do something positive; if you developed an effective strategy or tool, discovered something useful about the teaching/learning process, or gained an insight that had the potential to improve the conditions of others (i.e., students, families, services providers), you needed to produce scholarship, meaning publications and presentations. The synergy that could be realized between writing and presenting quickly became apparent. Although it was important to do both, I discovered that it was the written scholarship that had the most impact and longevity—so that is where I focused my efforts.

While conventional wisdom suggests that written scholarship becomes dated within about 5 years, I found that it often takes 8 to 12 years for the impact of a written product to peak (that is, be cited in the literature) and that high-quality scholarship can have a useful lifespan of well over 20 years. At least in my own field, this longevity effect exists because the status of attitudes, practices, and services is substantially different around the country and around the world. So what was new and relevant in 1994 in one locale may just be an emerging interest or need in another locale in 2014.

Understandably, there are conventions and standards within every academic discipline about what constitutes credible and acceptable scholarship. Within my own field, the gold standard is to get an article published in a highly regarded, peer-reviewed journal. In most cases, this means conforming to the style set forth by the American Psychological Association (APA) (2006). While APA conventions serve us well, and nothing in the written guidelines suggests that the content need be dry or boring, for the most part the genre of writing expected in most professional journals is technical reporting. While this may be essential to generate the body of evidence that helps build the theoretical foundations of our fields that ultimately are applied in practice, such technical genres are often crafted using discipline-specific and research jargon that can perpetuate insular exchanges. Ultimately, much of the professional literature is written by researchers for other researchers.

Although there is a valued place for this type of technical reporting, it may not effectively communicate with the audience that researchers in applied fields such as special education hope to inform, engage, and influence—including teachers, school leaders, and families. For a variety of additional reasons (e.g., lack of time, cost, access to subscription-based journals), field-based professionals and direct consumers simply do not keep up with the bounty of available literature. Applied fields have long recognized this problem and have had some success in developing differentiated outlets such as practitioner-oriented journals and books by trade publishers in an effort to bridge the gap between research and practice. Like many authors, I have also tried to get my work noticed by tinkering around the edges of tradition with catchy, alliterative, or provocative titles and attempted to make technical reporting more accessible by reducing the use of jargon and embedding more literary elements (e.g., stories, quotes, analogies, metaphors).

While these steps were satisfying and effective to some extent, they did not go far enough. Especially when presenting professionally, I was searching for ways to connect with my audience using visuals, stories, and humor. Having long been a fan of Gary Larsen's *Far Side* cartoons, I constantly searched his books and calendars for cartoon images that would help make my points. I would always find a few, but never enough, and rarely were they directly on point. Even so, the Larsen cartoons were effective presentation tools; people laughed and remained engaged long enough to consider the content of the research.

I often wished there were cartoons related to my own field to help me share its messages. I had seen cartoons about education, but too often they made fun of students or their parents. Such cartoons were antithetical to my aims, and I summarily rejected them. Professionals (including me at times) were the perpetrators of the absurd and damaging practices I witnessed throughout my career, not students and parents. It was these absurd professional behaviors I wanted to expose in the hopes of changing them. I also had seen some cartoons about disability, such as the work of John Callahan (1991). While I found much of his work compelling, insightful, and funny, some of it was too dark for my uses, not on-point to my topics of interest, or simply too R-rated for me to use in a public research presentation.

I ruminated on this gap in available cartoons for about 10 years before I finally began creating my own. Although incubating a problem is the norm in my working style, 10 years is a particularly long period of incubation, even for me. It may help to explain that a key reason I waited so long to commence cartooning is that I suffer from arrested development when it comes to drawing. I used to tell people it was arrested at the second-grade level, but I have since stopped doing that, realizing that it is potentially insulting to second-graders (many of whom have more advanced drawing skills than I do).

I guess it might be most accurate to refer to myself as a "semi-cartoonist." I can do part of the task, but not all of it. I can generate the images and text in my mind and sketch out the basic architecture of the cartoons, but it requires extensive explanation to understand many of my sketches. Even in those rare examples where my initial drafts are decipherable, they are not of a quality that I would want to share. I cannot draw facial expressions, actions, scaled sizes of anything, or distinguishable, four-legged animals. My attempts to draw a dog, goat, horse, mouse, or pig all look basically the same: a head, a torso, four legs, and a tail. I could not create by myself the cartoons that were so vivid in my mind's eye. My goal to develop cartoons to communicate research and issues in special education would require collaboration—specifically with someone who could draw! I had the good fortune of engaging the services of a talented and versatile artist, Kevin Ruelle, who runs a successful multi-media, commercial, and fine art business, Ruelle Design and Illustration, in Burlington, Vermont. We formed a successful collaboration and a friendship that now spans nearly 20 years and over 340 cartoons.

THE CREATIVE PROCESS

The creative process I used to transform ideas and notes into cartoons worthy of sharing actively relied on a variety of techniques drawn from the Osborn-Parnes Creative Problem-Solving (CPS) process (Osborn, 1993; Parnes, 1992, 1997). These include (a) *brainstorming*, a divergent, idea-generating process in which judgment is deferred in order to help stretch beyond the obvious to generate a quantity of ideas; (b) *forced relationships*, to search for connections and shared facts or observations between seemingly unrelated objects, concepts, or situations; and (c) *idea-joggers*, to manipulate ideas by minimizing, maximizing, rearranging, reversing, or eliminating elements. As Gordon and Poze (1979) explained, while learning occurs when we *make the strange familiar* (e.g., learning a foreign language), creativity and invention are facilitated when we purposely *make the familiar strange*. In combination with the aforementioned strategies, I employed analogies, associations, metaphors, paradoxes, and puns applied to issues and research findings about the field of special education to facilitate idea-generation, resulting in the cartoons.

The cartoon depicted in Figure 1.2 questions the wisdom of placing students in atypical environments (e.g., special education classes) and then requiring them to earn access to typical environments through their academic or behavioral achievement under atypical conditions. In Figure 1.3 the forced relationship method was used to highlight the desperation sometimes expressed by parents of children with disabilities in their quest to be heard by professionals.

Figure 1.2. Parole Approach.

Figure 1.3. Frequent Includer Program.

Once a draft was in good enough condition to share with the illustrator, we met, and I verbally described the picture in my head while referring to the rough draft. "You see this stick figure? That's a student sitting in a chair, shown from about the waist down. He is supposed to be fidgeting and squirming in his seat." The first cartoon I ever created was a commentary on the sometimes hasty, overzealous penchant for labeling any difference as disability (see Figure 1.4).

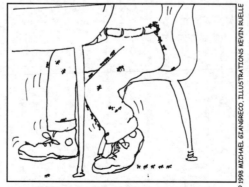

Figure 1.4. Ants in His Pants.

The illustrator then made a first attempt at redrawing the sketches based on the added description. We edited back and forth until the cartoon closely reflected the ideas represented in my original sketches and vision for the cartoon. Originally all the cartoons were black and white line drawings, because in 1998–2000, when the first three books of cartoons were published, the primary way visuals were displayed during presentations were on overhead transparencies. About that time, a shift was being made to computerized slide presentations. In response, we colorized all of the cartoons and made digital versions in both black and white and full color, available on searchable CD (Giangreco, 2007), so that people could more readily include the cartoons in their presentations.

DISSEMINATING SATIRICAL WORK

After generating enough cartoons to fill a book, it was time to secure a publisher—a task that would prove to be more difficult than anticipated. Having shown the cartoons to colleagues and having used them during several presentations, I was heartened that they were being well received by my intended audiences, and I felt confident that a savvy publisher would snatch them up quickly. I was wrong. Despite a complete mock-up of the first book to demonstrate its proposed layout, publisher after publisher rejected the cartoons. Their stated reasons spoke to the nature of what was deemed acceptable public discourse within the boundaries of academic publishing. Their concerns mostly centered on credibility and reputation, both theirs and mine. They wondered who would want the cartoons and how they would use them. They worried that some people might be offended by the content and sarcasm, and this could hurt their business. They wondered if their organization would be considered less scholarly if it added cartoons to its portfolio of publications. They speculated on whether disseminating cartoons would somehow tarnish my reputation as a scholar. There were few if any precedents for these academic publishers to guide their decision making when it came to this type of unconventional resource—especially one that openly poked fun at the absurdities of special education that pass as standard practice. Ultimately, over a dozen publishers (I lost exact count) decided that publishing satirical cartoons illuminating the foibles of special education was simply a risk they were unwilling to take.

Just when it seemed that every likely publisher had declined the opportunity to publish the first book of cartoons, persistence, luck, and good timing converged. A small, relatively new publisher located outside of Minneapolis, literally a "mom & pop" operation, decided to take a chance and publish the first book, *Ants in His Pants: Absurdities and Realities of Special Education* (Giangreco, 1998). Between 1998 and 2007, Peytral Publications published and successfully distributed four books of cartoons and a complete digital set on a searchable CD before Corwin Press (a SAGE Publications Company) acquired the rights to distribute the cartoons in 2007.

IMPACT OF CARTOONS

I must confess to a sense of satisfaction (and vindication) that many of the publishers who initially rejected the cartoons have since reprinted them in their books by other authors. To date, the cartoons have been reprinted in over 40 books, several journals, and countless newsletters disseminated by schools, parent groups, disability advocacy organizations, and professional associations. Authors have found ways to extend the reach of the cartoons by including them in books addressing a wide range of topics (e.g., advocacy, classroom management, collaboration, disability studies, diversity, inclusive education, early childhood education, law, literacy, media portrayals of disability, physical therapy, school administration, speech-language pathology, staff development, transition to adulthood, and universal design for learning). They are a staple at special education conferences and in university classroom presentations. They have been incorporated into staff development activities and displayed in state capitals to legislatures. They have been given as gifts, posted in offices and schools as reminders, and handed out as door prizes. Parents of children with disabilities have told me they have framed cartoons that closely reflected their own experiences and hung them in their homes or offices. Other parents and professionals have used them in meetings to help get their points across to colleagues. The cartoons can be used in innumerable creative ways.

Just as publishers had shied away from the cartoons, once they were published, so also did professional journals hesitate to write book reviews about the cartoons—maybe for some of the same reasons. The only leading journal that embraced the opportunity to offer a review was affiliated with the American Association on Intellectual and Developmental Disabilities. Journal editor Steven Taylor invited professor and editorial board member Scot Danforth to review the first two books of cartoons. Selected excerpts from his review speak to the value and potential impact of cartoons on public discourse. In part, Danforth (1999) wrote:

> But let me be serious about these cartoons, for although they split the reader's sides wide open, they are also very serious. As these cartoons lead us on a multi-barbed evaluation of the current state of special education in general and inclusive education in particular, we may take two pieces of advice from poet and literary critic T.S. Eliot. First, Eliot has reminded us that creativity and criticism go hand in hand. The critic's act of pulling apart

the familiar, turning it inside out, and rendering it odd and even ridiculous before our eyes is necessary to the creative process of developing new ideas and approaches. One cannot fashion the new without seriously questioning the old, without making what seems natural suddenly look absurd and in need of revision. Second, Eliot rightly pointed out that this creative and critical endeavor is rare, unpopular, and desirable. Few in any field of knowledge or work actually have the keenness of mind and the steeliness of stomach to engage in the creative work of serious criticism. Those few who do so are both necessary for the positive development of the field and intensely unpopular to the complacent multitude who prefer the comforting stasis of mediocrity to the uncertain and unsettling road of critique and innovation.

What Giangreco has done in these two cartoon volumes—working in the "theater of the mundane yet absurd" tradition of *The Far Side* and *Dilbert*—is hold up a stark mirror to our professional and organizational selves, inviting us to poke fun in harsh and even toxic tones, to see possibilities for a better world, to take responsibility for our professional lives. This cartoonist's quill is the scalpel of a skilled surgeon intent on making us squirm at an intensive examination of ourselves and our work.

We also must take note of the power of this humorous medium, the way a college professor can challenge a professional field with jokes in a manner probably not possible in typical academic writing. This fact should make us both appreciate the cartoonist's craft and question the moral usefulness of our typical professional discourse. By changing his role from "college professor" to "cartoonist," Giangreco arms himself with a discourse that moves beyond the jargoned stiffness of customary or "acceptable" professional writing and talk, positioning himself to safely lampoon much of what special education holds dear. He coaxes us in as awkwardly grinning accomplices, helping us to realize that the mirror held up before our profession bears the individual image of each of our faces. We are each responsible for the host of unsupportable practices and beliefs that are all too common in special education. We cannot help but bitterly smile that it is a cartoonist who is cajoling us into this realization. (Danforth, 1999, pp. 507–508)

Similar to other forms of publication, these cartoons continue to have longevity. Unfortunately, this may be because the issues and problems they address persist nationally and internationally. While the cartoons highlight various absurdities and realities, they are ultimately meant to encourage better educational practices (see Figure 1.5) by stimulating people to examine issues from different perspectives and encouraging creative ways to use them to improve education for children and youth. Hopefully, some of these cartoons might also bring a smile or laugh to people in the midst of tackling challenging conditions; we can sure use more of that in education to help grease the wheels of public discourse.

Figure 1.5. Clearing the Path.

REFERENCES

American Psychological Association. (2006). *Publication manual of the American Psychological Association* (6th ed.). Washington, DC: American Psychological Association.

Callahan, J. (1991). *Digesting the child within and other cartoons to live by.* New York: William Morrow.

Danforth, S. (1999). [Book Review of *Ants in his pants: Absurdities and realities of special education* (1998) and *Flying by the seat of your pants: Absurdities and realities of special education* (1999)]. *Mental Retardation, 37*(6), 507–508.

Giangreco, M.F. (1998). *Ants in his pants: Absurdities and realities of special education.* Thousand Oaks, CA: Corwin.

Giangreco, M.F. (1999). *Flying by the seat of your pants: More absurdities and realities of special education.* Thousand Oaks, CA: Corwin.

Giangreco, M.F. (2000). *Teaching old logs new tricks: Absurdities and realities of education.* Thousand Oaks, CA: Corwin.

Giangreco, M.F. (2002). *Absurdities and realities of special education: The best of ants…, flying…, and logs…* (Full color ed.). Thousand Oaks, CA: Corwin.

Giangreco, M.F. (2007). *Absurdities and realities of special education: The complete digital set* [CD]. Thousand Oaks, CA: Corwin.

Giangreco, M.F., Edelman, S., Luiselli, T.E., & MacFarland, S.Z. (1997). Helping or hovering? Effects of instructional assistant proximity on students with disabilities. *Exceptional Children, 64,* 7–18.

Gordon, W.J.J., & Poze, T. (1979). *The metaphorical way of learning and knowing.* Cambridge, MA: SES Associates.

Osborn, A.F. (1993). *Applied imagination: Principles and procedures of creative problem-solving* (3rd rev. ed.). Buffalo, NY: Creative Education Foundation Press.

Parnes, S.J. (Ed.). (1992). *Source book for creative problem-solving: A fifty-year digest of proven innovation processes.* Buffalo, NY: Creative Education Foundation Press.

Parnes, S.J. (1997). *Optimize the magic of your mind.* Buffalo, NY: Creative Education Foundation Press.

CHAPTER TWO

"Languaging Their Lives," Places of Engagement, and Collaborations with Urban Youth

VALERIE KINLOCH

INTRODUCTION

"Languaging Their Lives": A Reflective Poem

Eighteen-year-old Phillip –
    An intellectual, a knower, a provocative lyricist
With eighteen-year-old Khaleeq –
    A thinker, an innovator, a powerful meaning-maker.
Standing tall,
    Strong.
Standing full of words,
    Brave.
Standing with memories,
    History
Of family and friends,
Of neighbors present and
Neighbors displaced.
Standing in the presence of
        Community change,
        Gentrification.
        What they call, "a different type of Harlem."

Questioning meanings
    Of place,
    Of race,
    Of (un)belonging.
What Phillip describes as "unusual, like, who these new people?"
And what Khaleeq names "a new type of different that don't look like us."
Wondering what this change will bring –
    new condos we can't afford.
Talking about what this change will take away –
    the people who call this place home.
As they walk in search of meaning,
In pursuit of a place
They can continue to call home.

Because of Harlem,
For Harlem.
Why not in Harlem?
As they language their experiences,
Their lives,
Their ways of knowing
In a place that at once belongs to them
And at twice does not.

Two creative souls,
In one gentrifying community,
Languaging their lives
For you and for me.

I open this chapter with the above poem, "Languaging Their Lives," which I wrote after I participated in one of many literacy research sessions, over a span of 4 years, with Phillip and Khaleeq in New York City's Harlem community. On this particular day, Phillip conducted a community video walk-through session of familiar and unfamiliar sites in Harlem, and Khaleeq, Rebekkah (a university graduate student researcher), and I joined him. With a wide smile, Phillip proudly stood on the corner of 117th Street and Frederick Douglass Boulevard and pointed out to us some of the changes happening in, and to, his community: new stores, renovated apartments, expensive condominiums with balconies, and the increasing presence of White residents in the neighborhood. In the not-so-distant background of these changes were longstanding mom-and-pop corner stores, familiar street vendors, and semi-affordable, un-renovated apartments with fire escapes. Known for its history of civic, social, and political protest, Harlem has been a first or second home to many well-known African Americans whom we regularly discussed (e.g., Duke Ellington, Langston Hughes, and June Jordan), and it was the only home Phillip had ever known. As I stood alongside Rebekkah and as we watched both Phillip and Khaleeq masterfully maneuver the video cameras, I started thinking about recent conversations on urban gentrification we had had with Kim and Samantha, two of Phillip and Khaleeq's classmates at Harlem High School.

During an interview session in an empty classroom at the school, Phillip and I asked Kim and Samantha to share their impressions of Harlem with us. We asked them to "language their experiences." That is, we asked them to use words, signs, images, gestures, and any other type of oral, embodied, performative, and/or written expression to communicate their feelings about Harlem and the changes occurring there. In asking them to language their experiences, we were inviting them into a conversation about community that they came to narrate and that we came to listen to and learn from, intentionally and purposefully. The conversation began when Phillip asked, "How do you guys feel about your community?" Samantha's initial response was, "I don't know, like, I don't know. I think *they* waste their time on stuff that…on buildings and condos and stuff like that and *they* need to be working more on schools." She continued: "I don't understand why *they* make buildings in a community that is mostly filled with minorities…minorities around here don't have a lot of money like that to be living in no condos."

It became obvious that Samantha's use of the pronoun "they" was a reference to White people in financial positions of power or, to say it another way, with financial security. And while both Kim and Samantha elaborated on "they" throughout the interview, it was Phillip who eventually redirected the conversation away from an exclusive focus on White people to a discussion of the historical value of the community. When Kim and Samantha mentioned how they like to hang out on 125th Street and remember the good times they've had at the Apollo, Phillip encouraged them to think about Harlem's activists, artists, and cultural institutions. His encouragement reflected his ongoing efforts to engage in transformative work with his peers in and about this gentrifying community. As scholar Stephen Haymes (1995) asserts: "Because inner city blacks live on the margins of white supremacist domination and privilege, they have no other alternative but to struggle for the transformation of their places on the margin into spaces of cultural resistance" (p. 113). As Phillip listened to and talked with Kim and Samantha, it became apparent to me that they were struggling "for the transformation of their places" by languaging their lives into ongoing, "public" conversations (that they were not invited into) about a community that, for Khaleeq, represents "a new type of different that don't look like us."

At Phillip's insistence, Kim and Samantha shared what they know about Harlem—that people like Zora Neale Hurston, Malcolm X, and Adam Clayton Powell, Jr., had direct affiliations with Harlem, and that the Studio Museum of Harlem is an important community site. Before he talked about Harlem's renaissance era, Phillip asked them about their knowledge of the Schomburg Center, Hotel Theresa, and the Adam Clayton Powell, Jr., State Building. Instead of waiting for a response, Phillip quickly generated a list of reasons why Harlem's history, struggle, and beauty should be remembered in public attempts to gentrify the community. According to him, "Harlem's a historical landmark, look at the fights that went on right here for Black people's civil rights." He ended by saying:

> We gotta save Harlem from gentrification cause that's gonna displace poor and working people who live here. We gotta protect it from people who see it as a place to invest in building expensive condos that people here can't even afford. I'm just a concerned youth.

Observing Phillip over the span of our research project allowed me to witness his concern with what is already happening to Harlem because of urban gentrification and spatial reappropriation. Every time I think about his community video walk-through session, I return to lines from the poem that open this chapter: "Standing with memories, / *History*," or "Neighbors displaced," or "who these new people?" Then I think about Phillip as "an intellectual, a knower, a provocative lyricist" in light of how I come to represent him in writing to an audience that does not know him as I do and that may not be as familiar with his community as I am.

And this is my fear: that the words I use to describe Phillip, Khaleeq, Kim, Samantha, and other young adults are not enough, are too academic, and do nothing more than tell a story instead of incite change in how we see, work with, and learn from young people. The type of change I hope to incite is grounded in Haymes's (1995) focus on "spaces of cultural resistance" (p. 113), where we unapologetically fight against inequities and inequalities brought upon us because of racism, classism, sexism, linguistic homogeneity, spatial segregation, and the displacement of people from their homes and communities. As we create spaces of cultural resistance, I believe we must determine ways to work with young people in their communities and schools by inviting them to language their experiences. As they language their experiences, researchers must listen to what young people say and pay attention to what they do as we share lessons for action with a general public. In this way we are doing the work of a public intellectual, or a public scholar, because the young people we collaborate with are teaching us how to do the work and why the work is so important.

LANGUAGING AND PLACES OF ENGAGEMENT

> A youth of the community –
> *Maybe so, Val. Maybe so.*
> A youth for the community –
> *I'm just trying to help save Harlem.*

He is concerned about the community because
> *I care about what's gonna happen.*
His concern for the community means
> *Being engaged, learning more and more everyday. Figuring out what*
I can do.

Yet he fears that his words and actions
Won't be taken seriously
By those who look upon him
With questioning eyes.

You are for the community, I ask.
I'm for the community, he replies,
Because I am
A concerned youth.

In his concern exists tension –
> *Not everybody gonna understand why I'm doing this work.*
In his concern exists struggle –
> *I walk into school and nobody's talking about what's happening out there*
in here.
> *And you know what, Val,*
> *I learn more from the community…than from schools.*
He asks me about community engagement
And we talk about relationships, collaborations, action,
Changing the world.

About organizing, revolutionizing, making space for many voices,
Changing the world.
> *We gotta do this in the community and in the schools, Val.*
And I tell him, we already doing this, Phillip.
Changing the world.

We already doing this.
He tells me to call our work "places of engagement" because
> *We gotta do this in the community and in the schools, Val.*
Changing the world.

How do we heed Phillip's advice to "do this in the community and in the schools" as we simultaneously seek to create (and to call our work) "places of engagement"? Inherent in Phillip's assertions is his awareness that unknown others might look upon him with questioning eyes, wondering what he is doing with a video camera in one hand and a journal and pen in the other. He is also aware that many of those looks have less to do with what he is carrying in his hands and more to do with who he is: a young, Black male from an urban community who wears t-shirts and baggy jeans and who meshes his linguistic registers with "academic" English and African American Language (AAL). And these descriptors alone don't do justice to *who* Phillip is and why he cares about his community. These descriptors don't emphasize why he seeks to be "engaged, learning more and more everyday. Figuring out what I can do."

There is no question to me that Phillip is languaging his experiences in places of engagement that encourage him to seek relationships and collaborations, to organize and revolutionize, and to take action to change the world. His languaging is represented by how he (1) communicates with his peers (e.g., Kim, Samantha, Khaleeq, and others) to question urban gentrification; (2) talks about voicing his experiences and "making space for many [other] voices"; (3) seeks to make a difference in the world not only for himself, but for an entire community (e.g., I'm just trying to help save Harlem); and (4) documents—orally, digitally, and in print—the before (his acknowledgment of the past), the during (his desire to remember the present), and the after (his questioning of the future) of gentrification. His languaging points to his struggles for cultural resistance against dominance, power, and unwarranted change which, in this case, go by the name gentrification. Instead of gentrification, which oftentimes comes with harsh realities for longtime community residents, Phillip seeks places of engagement that explicitly involve schools and communities working together to change the world. When I asked Phillip to talk about his vision for places of engagement, he shared the following:

> Like places of engagement.
> These places where
> We be workin' together,
> Like, learn and, well, grow together.
> I learn from you 'cause
> You learn from me.
> And, see,
> Like, we got respect for each other
> In the process.
>> *So, in these places of engagement,*
>> *There's reciprocity?*
>> *Is that what I'm hearing, Phil?*
> OK, look:
> We got that, yeah,
> We got trust,
> People listenin' to the next person,
> Learning together.
>> *In schools and communities, or…?*

> Anywhere, Val!
> And, like, because of all that
> We naturally engaging each other.
> You put this engagement in different places,
> That's the action.
> Good things happen.
> > *I like your places of engagement a lot.*
> It's not **my** places, Val,
> It's **ours.**
> Ours.

Phillip's concept of "places of engagement" is important in that it brings to life his earlier sentiment that "we all have a place in the world…so we all gotta help make the change." Together, these ideas further emphasize how places of engagement belong to us—they aren't "my places," but "ours."

This narrative of engagement, collaboration, and change does not often get assigned to Black male youth in urban schools and communities. Popular assumptions about Black youth, specifically, and urban youth, generally, and how they language their experiences often ignore how they work in (and for) the local community, how they adopt an activist stance to question inadequate living conditions, and how they collaborate with others to make the world a more socially, civically, politically, and educationally just place in which to live and learn. These images, however, should come to mind. They should be what we think about when we walk into schools and enter into young people's communities. Importantly, these images and the ensuing youth narratives about places of engagement, collaboration, and languaging should be at the heart of all educational debates that purport to advantage *best practices, core standards, testing, unnecessary tracking,* and *achievement,* but they are not. Because they aren't, we have no other choice but to redirect educational conversations and the language used to describe students in urban schools and communities from acts of dehumanization ("those kids can't learn"; "just build more prisons") to practices in humanization ("students have agency"; "students teaching other students and their teachers"; "build more schools"). Both Haymes's (1995) "cultural resistance" and Phillip's "places of engagement" are crucial components of this work.

LANGUAGING AND COLLABORATIONS WITH URBAN YOUTH

> We be working and
> You be out here with us, Val.
> How you define gentrification?

'Cause you know, you be listening to us,
And now we wanna listen to how you,
You know,
Like, define gentrification.

You know you agree with us
'Cause you be, like,
You be really listening.
I wanna learn to do that thing you do, Val.
    What thing?
Like, you know, how you listen to us like that.
You really be listening.

Yeah, you do.
    Well, y'all got important stuff to say,
    Why wouldn't I wanna listen
    To you?
    Y'all deep.
Yeah, we deep!
But we still wanna know
How you define gentrification.
Val be trippin'.

I did eventually come to define gentrification similar to how Phillip, Khaleeq, and their peers defined it—the changing and corporatization of community space that often result in the displacement of longtime community residents. And, in the case of Harlem, many of those residents are Black and Brown people. For us, this definition also encapsulates efforts in place-taking, that is, the taking of physical forms of familial, cultural, social, and educational spaces from a group of people whose perspectives are not directly included in decision-making processes. When I shared my definition with Phillip and Khaleeq, they poked, "You agree with us? We taught you that? Was it the other way around, Val?"

Indeed, they taught me that and so many other things about community, activism, voice, literacy, and language. They taught me how to "really be listening" to what they say and do not say, and to pay close attention to the silences and action that get tagged on to the movements of their bodies throughout the community and the school. They also reminded me that not everyone takes them seriously and that not everyone listens to what they have to say. Thus, as I work toward creating and sustaining Phillip's places of engagement, I must also recognize that not everyone seeks such places and that not everyone will listen. This point comes through so poignantly in the following exchange among Phillip, Khaleeq, and me:

Phillip: You think people gonna listen
             To us? Think about that.

Khaleeq: They not taking us for real,
             Like we not serious.

Valerie: Why you think that?

Phillip: This for real work we doing, Val,
             You know that.
             The issue is,
             Whose story is going to be told?

Khaleeq: He right!

As I engage in the work of languaging and collaborating with urban youth, I take seriously Phillip's sentiments that "this for real work we doing," and I wonder why some people are quick to read their work in the community as an uncritical extracurricular activity. Maybe it is fear that drives such comments from onlookers. Or maybe it is an unwillingness to change the negative discourse of schooling and engagement that has gotten tacked onto one too many urban youth. As I take seriously Phillip's comment, I also grapple with Khaleeq's belief that "they not taking us for real," and I wonder why. How can Phillip and Khaleeq not be taken "for real" when they assert so much agency in languaging their experiences, especially as they come to name what they see *of* the community as "a different type of Harlem" and "a new type of different that don't look like us?" As I consider the whys, I return to my fear that I might not sufficiently represent to other people the literacies and languages of Phillip, Khaleeq, Kim, Samantha, and the other young people with whom I collaborate. What is the language that I should use as I attempt to convey the nuances of this work to an unknowing and, possibly, an unforgiving audience? How do I adequately describe the complexities of their identities and their desire to make the world a better place than how they found it? How do I ethically, honestly, and bravely answer Phillip's question, "Whose story is going to be told?"

From working with young people in schools and communities, I have learned that the language I use to write and talk about our work must humanize us. It must reflect how we individually and collectively language our experiences, how we interact in places of engagement, and how we collaborate with each other across shifting contexts. Essentially, it must account for the myriad ways in which we are all knowers and doers. In these ways, then, we not only envision but also create places of engagement that take up the work of cultural resistance. In turn, I am a public scholar because Phillip and Khaleeq are public scholars and community ethnographers.

LANGUAGING AND THE WORK OF A PUBLIC SCHOLAR

What does this work mean for how public scholars can collaborate with young people as they language their experiences in community spaces? Additionally, what larger implications does this work have for how educational researchers as public scholars represent the language, literacies, and activist stances of young people to a public audience? As I reflect on these questions through the examples I've shared, I return to how I opened this chapter—by describing Phillip as "an intellectual, a knower, a provocative lyricist" and Khaleeq as "a thinker, an innovator, a powerful meaning-maker." Hidden within these descriptions are the layers upon layers of other descriptions that have been placed upon both Phillip and Khaleeq through-out their adolescent and young adult years. As they name them, these *other(ed)* descriptions range from "lazy and too loud" to "nice but not smart enough." There is anger in their voices and disappointment on their faces. So I listen and I look. There is a commitment to reject the narratives of failure placed upon them. So I listen and I look. There is frustration in their talk of how schools aren't addressing community issues. So I listen and I look. There is also an urgency to talk, plan, take action, and make positive change happen now. And so I listen and I look. In my acts of listening and looking, I seek to get closer and closer to knowing Phillip and Khaleeq as engaged community members whose lived experiences and cultural ways of knowing are intricately connected to their "places of engagement."

With my acts of listening and looking comes action. I collaborate with Phillip and Khaleeq to discover new ways to disrupt the negative, pervasively dangerous descriptions that have been placed upon them and their peers. A part of this dis-ruption requires me to be present with them in community spaces as we learn with and from one another. In the community, we ask each other hard questions about racism, gentrification, and struggle, and we recall memories from our various childhoods that we associate with particular people, places, and events. Another part of this work requires me to seek out invitations to witness who they are inside school. Observing them in their English classroom, in the hallways and stairwells, in the teachers' lounge, and throughout the other spaces of the school building provided me with an expanded way of seeing who they are, how they perform identities, and how they respond to social issues.

Another important part of this disruption requires me to use language that represents, in humanizing ways, aspects of who they are—individually and collectively—and of the work we do. Test scores and grades, for instance, can never fully—if at all—characterize the sheer brilliance and academic and social acuity of

Phillip, Khaleeq, Kim, Samantha, and their peers. By not including the personal stories of young people in larger educational conversations, I fear that the public will not understand that young people are already engaged scholars, activists, and ethnographers. Thus, it becomes my ongoing responsibility to write about young people in ways that showcase who they are, how they see the world, how they seek to change the world, and how they, in fact, are working to interrogate public narratives about urban schools, communities, and young people that are too often driven by deficit perspectives and not by humanizing, assets-based orientations.

This is the work that I do. It is the work I am dedicated and committed to, day in and day out. And it is the work that other educational researchers and/as public scholars do. For we are aware of the challenges confronting many youth of color in urban schools and communities throughout the United States, and in our awareness, we talk back to inequitable structures, systems, and practices that marginalize, dehumanize, and criticize young people. As we talk back, we can come to language our experiences in relation to how young people language their experiences in communities and schools. For me, the ways in which I write about the lived conditions, identities, and epistemological perspectives of young people (and myself) for a public audience are highly influenced by how and why we language our experiences in relation to larger educational, political, and civic concerns. We seek to change the world by creating and sustaining places of engagement in which we can openly and honestly talk about the many challenges facing people of color in urban contexts. From gentrification and displacement to racism and inequitable educational structures, our work is personal just as much as it is political. In fact, our work and the languaging of our experiences are acts of resistance against, as Stephen Haymes (1995) tells us, "domination and privilege" and for "spaces of cultural resistance" (p. 113; see also hooks, 1999).

How I come to represent this work to a public audience, then, becomes a major concern and struggle for me. I am honest about my struggle with Phillip, Khaleeq, and the other young people with whom I collaborate. In my writings (as with this chapter), I include a combination of data from my researcher journals and field notes, from participant interviews, from community video walk-through sessions, and from analysis of data that comes directly from me and from project participants-as-collaborators (see Kinloch, 2010, 2012). Doing these things demonstrates a level of care and respect we have for each other that allows us not only to talk about what we see happening (or not) in school and community contexts, but to language our experiences as we create, sustain, and include others in *our* places of engagement.

So, when I think I do not have the language to represent the work we are doing to a public audience, I look into the knowing eyes of Phillip and Khaleeq. When I think others will not understand that the work we do in the community and that we take back into the high school is so very important, I remember that it is meaningful for the young people who willingly, openly, and voluntarily work with me, challenge me, and remind me to keep going. Just as much as the work is meaningful to them, it is meaningful to me and for me. Finally, when I think about the work we do against the backdrop of the work of a public scholar—and the challenges with making our work available and accessible to others—I think, "Why not?" Why not work against and work to resist the racist, classist narratives of failure and underachievement that others have come to associate with so many urban youth and adults of color? Why not, as if I have a choice to do otherwise? As if I have a right not to do this work. For not doing this work is to not remember our history full of honor, bravery, and determination on the one hand, and of struggle, strife, and abuse on the other. Also, to not do this work is to not understand, accept, and know that we are all connected, one unto the other. Or, according to the popular South African term, Ubuntu, my humanity is your humanity, for "I am because you are."

Hence I am a public scholar because the young people with whom I collaborate are public scholars who are languaging their experiences in places of engagement. As they language their experiences, so do I. And as we language our experiences with each other, we gain a deeper understanding of who we are, of the work we do, and of the challenges that we must continuously work against in making our work available to a public audience. In closing, it is Phillip who reminds me of the following:

> We gotta do this work
> We don't have a choice
> When I ask you—*Whose story is going to be told? –*
> I ask because we gotta make sure
> That we being real about this
> How we decide to talk about
> Our work
> It's like important
> And other people need to know that, Val.

AUTHOR'S NOTE

A big thanks to Phillip, Khaleeq, Kim, Samantha, their peers, and their teachers at Harlem High School as well as members of the local community for collaborating on this research project. Also, I am indebted to the Spencer Foundation and the National Council of Teachers of English for supporting aspects of this research project.

REFERENCES

Haymes, S. (1995). *Race, culture, and the city: A pedagogy for Black urban struggle.* Albany: State University of New York Press.

hooks, b. (1999). *Yearning: Race, gender, and cultural politics.* New York: South End Press.

Kinloch, V. (2010). *Harlem on our minds: Place, race, and the literacies of urban youth.* New York: Teachers College Press.

Kinloch, V. (2012). *Crossing boundaries—Teaching and learning with urban youth.* New York: Teachers College Press.

CHAPTER THREE

Reframing

We Are Not Public Intellectuals; We Are Movement Intellectuals

MARGARITA MACHADO-CASAS, BELINDA BUSTOS FLORES,
AND ENRIQUE MURILLO, JR.

The definition of the term "public" has expanded with increased access to the Internet, and scholars have begun to engage in an examination of contemporary academics as public intellectuals. Vásquez, Flores, and Clark (2013) remind us that: "It does not happen very often that three scholars who do not typically communicate with each other, approach a creative alliance in search of a common goal" (p. 111). In defining our role within the wider public sphere, we followed Vásquez et al.'s (2013) example for approaching the task "without hidden agendas and tripping all over each other's self-importance" (p. 111). As we pondered the question of "Are we public intellectuals? How do we see ourselves? And how do we define what we do for our communities both academically and socially? We recognized the mutual respect and collegiality we had for one another. Moreover, we realized that although we knew each other's work, we had not taken the opportunity to reflect on the collective impact and the wide-recognition we have achieved for our work as both change agents and scholars.

Compromiso y Necesidad de Ver Cambio

Our work has been driven by *compromiso y necesidad de ver cambio* (commitment and the necessity to see change) embodied in a desire to make a difference in the educational success of culturally and linguistically diverse children and students in the United States. It did not take us long to recognize that the vectors of our research agendas converge into one goal, one mind approached from three different directions as we outline below.

Dr. Murillo is a first-generation Chicano, born and raised in Eastside Los Angeles, and a native bilingual speaker in Spanish/English and a full professor at California State University, San Bernardino. Dr. Murillo currently serves as executive director and founder of the LEAD organization (Latino Education & Advocacy Days), whose objective is to promote a broad-based awareness of the crisis in Latino education and to enhance the intellectual, cultural, and personal development of our community's educators, administrators, leaders, and students. LEAD has become a staple in Latino education in the United States and has reached millions here and abroad. Dr. Murillo is also the founding editor of the *Journal of Latinos and Education*, former commissioner of the California Student Aid Commission, and founder of the National Latino Education Network.

Dr. Flores, a first-generation college student from the barrios of San Antonio, graduated from the University of Texas and is currently a full professor and chair of the Bicultural-Bilingual Studies Department at UTSA. In 2003, she founded the Academy for Teacher Excellence (ATE) at the University of Texas at San Antonio (UTSA). As ATE's principal investigator, she has secured over $17 million to recruit, prepare, and retain Latinos and other minorities in critical teacher shortage areas such as bilingual education, mathematics, science, and special education. To provide educational opportunities along the pre-K–20 continuum, she has designed, implemented, and studied various innovative research-based projects such as La Clase Mágica (patterned after Vásquez's [2003] afterschool technology-integration program) and iCLASS: Innovative Community of Learning Advancing Student Success (early college for Latino youth). Collaborative partnerships formed across the university and with external entities have been critical to ensuring ATE's success and efforts. In 2012, Dr. Flores was inducted into the San Antonio Women's Hall of Fame and was selected as the Texas Association for Bilingual Education Higher Education Honoree.

Dr. Margarita Machado-Casas is an associate professor at UTSA. She is the co-creator and chair of the first-ever national Bilingual Education Student Organization (BESO) for the National Association of Bilingual Educators (NABE), which includes more than 25 universities and over 300 undergraduate and graduate education students. She is the co-creator of several multilingual and multiethnic language master's programs across Latin America and the co-creator of the TransAfroLat Education Network, which connects scholars and students throughout Latin America and some parts of Europe who are engaged in the study of education, foundation, plurality, and social justice for linguistically and ethnically diverse groups across the globe. Dr. Machado-Casas is also the co-director of the National Education Latino network, which provides educational links to over half a million people around the world. She is also a contributor to the Latino Education Advocacy Days (LEAD) and the co-director of the National Latino Education Network (NLEN), which brings educational communities from across the globe together once a year for an education conference.

Given our aforementioned commitment to improve the educational success of culturally and linguistically diverse children and students in the United States, when asked to write a piece on how we negotiate our roles as public intellectuals, we began to think about this term and felt uneasy about its connotations and the role these definitions hold for scholars and educators. After some critical reflection on our own varied roles and commitments, we came to the conclusion that we do not consider ourselves "public intellectuals"; instead, we feel that we are "movement intellectuals," and we explain our reasoning below. We have identified three ways in which we see ourselves as movement intellectuals: (1) recognizing that our communities are not *tabula rasae*, (2) reframing dominant spheres and creating alternatives public spheres, and (3) creating alternative spaces for the social construction of knowledge.

MOVEMENT INTELLECTUALS

Examinations of contemporary debates about public intellectuals often focus on the need for action (Abascal-Hildebrand, 1999). Other scholars can trace the term "engaged intellectual' to the early nineteenth century to describe the intellectuals who were vocal in their criticism of the state's conduct around the trial and the reaction of civil society (Sadri, 1992). Additionally, researchers have stated that the main goal of public individuals is to draw attention to competing claims of the relationship between the academy/students/schooling and public life. Cushman (1999) argues that the main issue with the term "public intellectuals" is the use of the term "public," because it pertains to middle-to-upper-class policymakers, administrators, and politicians. As such, it is subtractive, because it does not allow for the public to be a site for unity and knowledge with the ultimate goal of highlighting the "need to draw attention to the obligation and necessity to call for action" (p. 329). Perhaps these countering views demonstrate our differing philosophies as to our roles as movement intellectuals compared to the existing definitions—we simply do not fit these paradigms.

Recognizing That Our Communities Are Not Tabula Rasae

For years, many have "called for action" and have tried to raise awareness of the issues affecting our communities. And although we feel that our work *is* a call to action, we believe that simply calling for action is not enough. It is no more than a vicious cycle of perpetuated limbo that oftentimes detracts from its very purpose—action. Furthermore, we begin with the realization that there are many instances of action within our communities. We recognize that the struggle has been a longstanding one, and much has been and is being done in communities on a smaller scale to make a difference. Our communities are not blank slates; individuals are, rather, actors in the transformation of our communities. Unfortunately, these isolated invisible acts go unrecognized because these individuals have been ostracized from the dominant social sphere. We are fully aware that the action is there in many forms. Examples include the Communities Organized for Public Services (COPS) in San Antonio, Texas, and numerous other organizations in California and across the United States. This is why acknowledging this grassroots efforts and the "sacred knowledge" of our communities (Flores, Vásquez, & Clark, 2014) is critical in our work and our conceptualization as movement intellectuals.

Reframing Dominant Spheres

As academics, rather than calling for and teaching about action, we reframed our role in creating a movement—a public awareness—that recognizes and bolsters grassroots efforts by bringing these to the dominant social sphere. Therefore, our role as movement intellectuals is to work in/within/against dominant social spheres to purposely alter the status quo through creative activities in the collective social construction of knowledge. According to Vásquez and fellow researchers (2013):

> Rather than leading to "shared voices and visions" (John-Steiner, 2000, p. 5), this action has created a reaction that "led to a re-articulation of a marginalized existing voice and vision present in a "cultural and historical milieu" that historically has disregarded minority epistemologies and contributions to the development of the "American" nation-state. (p. 112)

In doing so, we are "coyotes" (Murillo, 1999) within a dominant "whitestream" (Segura, 1989) social sphere not typically designed for the inclusion of minority communities and their needs. We are bridge builders and connectors of active—albeit at times silent—small national and international movements, creating collective alternative spaces, claiming them, duplicating them, and finding new ways to make them part of the dominant social sphere. It is the idea that we can no longer hide, and we will not abide to hegemonic and oppressive forces. Whereas public intellectuals may make themselves explicitly and politically relevant to some portion of the public, a movement intellectual is more likely not to have taken on the significance of being publicly relevant at all in the dominant sphere, as he or she proceeds from a different set of assumptions. Moreover, a movement intellectual's "intellectual life" as the colonized working within the colonizer's hegemonic institution, is more often in contrast to the privatized bureaucratic professional roles, types of thinking, activities and outlook as university faculty, as it may require one to rise above the preoccupations of one's own profession. The three of us reside in higher education institutions, and we are criticized—often for good reason—for our tendency to isolate ourselves from our surrounding contexts and for not being more engaged with the issues that affect the communities in which we are located. As movement intellectuals, we fundamentally agree that there are important issues that directly or indirectly affect institutions and the multiple communities we straddle that require us to "climb out of the ivory tower," to do the action work that is most relevant to our local contexts and publics.

Creating Alternative Spaces for the Social Construction of Knowledge

Through our efforts, both independent and collective, we are building a bridge for current local, national, and international networks to become part of these micro and macro movements and creating new ones for the social construction of knowledge and the improvement of our communities. So, rather than leading to "shared voices and visions" (John-Steiner, 2000, p. 5), as public individuals we are creating alternative spaces within dominant public spheres. Movement intellectuals on the front lines collaborate and invite teamwork to overcome challenges. Explicit commentary may sometimes embrace dissonance, conflict, and divergent thinking as part of constructive change, to help people change their field of perception, to see why they should commit to doing something differently—to be part of transformation and to expand one's context and method, thereby adding visibility, voice, and presence in the dominant public sphere through a collective network. Each of us has been able to transform the system and create these alternative spaces that lead to the knowledge construction by (1) being inclusive of others, (2) assuming culpability, and (3) doing our work, not justifying it.

Inclusivity, Culpability, Doing Our Work, Not Justifying It!

Part of what we have been able to do in our own spaces is create opportunities for others to be heard and seen. This work is threefold: (1) we provide opportunities and space for others to get involved; (2) we build relationships with entities that do not often work together; and (3) we model the ways in which others can do the same in their own communities. Thus, our work challenges the "unstated practice of privileging individual production over collaborative work [that] is one of those well-understood agendas that make up the hidden curriculum" in academia (Vásquez et al., 2013, p. 113). Margarita's own experience is a good example of how this is done. She herself is partly a product of the way in which others, including

Enrique and Belinda, have been inclusive and good role models for keeping this movement going. Margarita began working on the *Journal of Latinos in Education* as a master's-level student at CSUSB and was part of the initial efforts to get it started.

> I passed out flyers, helped organize the first couple Latinos in Education events at the American Educational Studies Association (AESA) and American Educational Research Association (AERA), and later came on board with other projects such as the *Handbook of Latinos in Education* and LEAD. Meanwhile, with this example, I was able to understand the necessity of navigating different spaces and being inclusive, and began working on my research and movement agenda. Such examples include: working with international institutions and grassroots in the United States and abroad, creating programs and then bringing them back to movements in the United States, including bringing connections to LEAD and expanding the notions of involvement to an international multidisciplinary approach by looking at the issues globally and including others abroad.

At UTSA, Margarita had the opportunity to work with Belinda, who invited her to join the Academy for Teaching Excellence team, in a collective movement. At the same time she was able to create new projects for the community involving both media and community groups.

> I was able then to connect this to the international efforts and to LEAD and together we are now working on expanding our roles as movement intellectuals. Now, as it was done to me—I'm passing the baton to others I encounter with the international projects through the TransAfroLat Education Network.

As minority scholars and leaders, we assume this responsibility to map out the path; we cannot expect others to do it. While some may see this as a burden, we recognize that what we do not only impacts us as individuals but also affects the group. Thus, unlike some who seek power or want to wield power, we recognize that transformation requires vision, leadership, and sociocultural understanding. As minority faculty, we have a distinct view of the world and an understanding of the possibilities that this change can bring for the betterment of our communities. As an organic effort, it is socially constructed and experientially framed.

As Belinda reflects: "I have long recognized that to create movement, you have to have a vision, find those who are like-minded, and create a resolve to challenge the status quo." But for a movement to be realized, you must be willing to listen to the voices of others, and you must move forward. For every challenge, your realized work and that of others provides the counter-example. As academics, this requires that we create an environment within and outside our communities in which others move the agenda forward and, ultimately, results in the desired action.

CONCLUSION

We can no longer afford to simply engage in discourse about inequities, and while much has been accomplished through our collective efforts, we are standing at a precipice. There is still much work to be done, and we call on our colleagues to create spaces in which the knowledge, wisdom, and voices of our communities are heard, understood, and valued. Concomitantly, these spaces must allow for the construction of knowledge and the transformation of the public spheres.

REFERENCES

Abascal-Hildebrand. (1999). Narrative and the Public Intellectual. *Educational Studies.* 30(1), 5–18.

Cushman, E. (1999). The public intellectual, service learning, and activist research. *College English*, *61*, 328–336.

Flores, B.B., Vásquez, O.A., & Clark, E.R. (2014). *Generating transworld pedagogy: Reimagining la clase mágica.* Lanham, MD: Lexington Books.

John-Steiner, V. (2000). *Creative collaborations.* New York: Oxford University Press.

Murillo, Jr., E.G. (1999). Mojado crossings along neoliberal borderlands. *Educational Foundations*, *13*(1), 7–30.

Sadri, A. (2000). *Max Weber's Sociology of Intellectuals.* New York: Oxford University Press.

Segura, D.A. (1989). Chicana and Mexican immigrant women at work: The impact of class, race, and gender on occupational mobility. *Gender and Society*, *3*, 37–52.

Vásquez, O.A. (2003). *La clase mágica: Imagining optimal possibilities in a bilingual community of learners.* Mahwah, NJ: Lawrence Erlbaum.

Vásquez, O.A., Flores, B.B., & Clark, E.R. (2013). *Consejos: Un diálogo respetoso:* A critical and respectful dialogue. *Journal of Social Foundations*, *27*(1–2), 111–118.

CHAPTER FOUR

Scholarly Personal Narrative as a Way to Connect the Academy to the World

ROBERT J. NASH

INTRODUCTION

I remember vividly the day I received an email from the editors of this volume. It was an invitation to submit a chapter on the "public intellectual." They also encouraged me to write in a first-person narrative style. Both of them knew that, in the 1990s, I created a way of doing research that I call Scholarly Personal Narrative writing (or SPN). Since then I have authored four books (Nash, 2004; Nash & Bradley, 2011; Nash & Viray, 2013, 2014) on what I call "Me-Search/Re-Search" writing. Of course I jumped at the opportunity to write about using SPN as a way to bridge the gap between scholars, students, and the general public. I have been trying to make the case for doing this for many years. I am grateful to my editors for the chance to sum up much of my writing about SPN, as well as to be able to enrich my thinking about what it is to be an SPN public intellectual.

For me, Scholarly Personal Narrative (SPN) is a style of public-intellectual writing based in storytelling and self-disclosure, one that draws from a variety of academic and non-academic references and findings. It allows the writer to communicate to a non-academic audience the excitement of the intellectual life in a way that is accessible and creative, and that realistically reflects the complexities of daily life and personal identity. In this chapter I hope to make a case for communicating both the spirit and the findings of academic research and scholarship to non-faculty constituencies in a way that is attractive and inspiring. I will propose a connective way of writing—Scholarly Personal Narrative—that makes the cross-over from the esoteric to the vernacular without sacrificing intellectual integrity for general accessibility. And I will try to do all of this in a personal, narrative writing style. Therefore, this is most decidedly not meant to be a "tenure article." On the contrary, my intent is to make it comprehensible to all—not just to the professorial guild.

WHAT THE TERM PUBLIC INTELLECTUAL MEANS TO ME

I love what I do. I am in the enviable position of being a veteran, tenured, award-winning full professor who can publicly profess a belief in, and a love for, ideas and people without worrying about gaining tenure, promotion, or national distinction. I am an interdisciplinary philosopher, a religious studies scholar, an ethicist, a creative writing instructor, a social justice "gladvocate" (Nash, Johnson, & Murray, 2012), a cosmopolite, a moral conversationalist, and an etymological wordsmith. I teach all of these subjects, and I do so with enthusiasm and excitement. I am convinced that I can make a difference in the lives of my students and, by extension, the lives of all those people my students know. I have evolved over a faculty career of 46 years from being someone who wanted to be seen as erudite and whose work was accessible only to a select few to someone who wants to be understood, and inspiring, to everyone—both on and off campus. I think of myself as a meaning-making mentor for the quarterlife generation and for all the generations afterward. I want to become a writer, speaker, and teacher who is able to convey his truths in a language that is non-elitist, non-technical, and non-authoritarian. This is what I mean when I use the phrase "public intellectual."

It does not follow, however, that I am intent on "dumbing down" my subject matter. ("Dumbing down" implies a pontifical judgment that some people are unable to understand academic ideas, and, therefore, oversimplification is necessary for their sake.) Neither does it mean that I disdain specialized terminology or complex ideas. I am enough of an interdisciplinary thinker who loves ideas and who has written, taught, and talked about these ideas throughout my professional life to want to share what I know and value with as many people as I can. I want to enlarge my audiences to include not just my students and colleagues but also friends in my neighborhood, people from the larger non-university community who attend my lectures and presentations, and those in a number of helping professions who seek my services as an ethics, writing, meaning-making, and communications consultant. I am certain of one thing at this late stage in my career: I will no longer waste my time strutting my professorial stuff in order to prove my "superior" intellectual prowess. This is the way I used to live in academia. At this time in my life, though, I strive to be a public intellectual who connects, rather than separates, ideas and people. I want to learn as much from everyone I meet as they might be able to learn from me. I call this "reciprocity teaching and learning." This is what I believe SPN writing is all about: it is connective writing at its best.

It is important to understand that the word "intellectual" has two meanings that date all the way back to ancient Greece. One of these has to do with being able to perceive and understand the world both rationally *and* emotionally; in this sense, then, an intellectual is pluralistic, multi-faceted, and holistic in the search for wisdom, purpose, and meaning (Anderson, 1992; Graff, 2003). Socrates, Plato, and Aristotle were holistic intellectuals who walked among the people without favoring one group over another. They welcomed all to join them in their pursuit of wisdom. The other definition of "intellectual" has to do with possessing a superior mental ability that is almost always rational and cognitive. Sadly, this type of intellectual sometimes comes off as exclusive, skeptical, overly analytical, and hyper-specialized. The message that the intellectual exclusivist sends to those outside the "club" is this: you may choose to learn from me if you wish, but you are neither qualified nor worthy to join my guild until you become like me.

I do not want to be an intellectual exclusivist, even though I was trained to wear this mask. I am here instead to be a genuine philosopher—someone who loves the pursuit of wisdom as well as someone who loves all those who pursue wisdom; someone who is intellectual in the sense of learning from everyone's experiences no matter how ordinary or extraordinary; and someone who has spent his entire career learning how to reason with both his head *and* his heart. I am pleased to say that after 46 years in higher education, my heart is just now beginning to catch up with my head. But at times—especially when I am "performing" at a professional conference or at a departmental faculty meeting—the distance between the two is still vast, I'm afraid. Most important for me, however, a "public intellectual" cares greatly about being able to communicate with *all* audiences—both public and private, on-campus and off-campus, degreed and non-degreed.

WHAT ALL OF US HAVE IN COMMON THROUGHOUT THE WORLD: THE NEED TO MAKE MEANING OF OUR LIVES BY TELLING OUR STORIES

During the four and one-half decades I have been a professor, I have yet to meet a single person, either inside or outside my classroom, who is impervious to what I consider to be *the* major survival human need: *making meaning and becoming a whole person by telling his or her story*. In fact, for Hayden White (1987), a literary historian, the word "narrative" derives from the ancient Sanskrit "gna," a root term that means "know," "tell," and even, by extension, "survive." Moreover, this is an innate evolutionary drive, according to such experts as H. Porter Abbott, Jerome Bruner, and Paul J. Eakin (see Abbot, 2002). For some evolutionary theorists, there are few human practices that have as much adaptive value as the human instinct to tell—and to hear—stories about meaning-making.

SPN writing begins, continues, and ends with storytelling. Stories provide the opportunity to write our way to meaning and wholeness inside and outside the academy. As we in higher education enter the twenty-first century, I believe it is a necessity for us to update our approaches to research and teaching by encouraging our students, and our colleagues, to write their personal stories. I want to help others—my students, colleagues, and friends—to *write* their way into meaning and wholeness. In fact, this is the primary purpose of Scholarly Personal Narrative writing as I teach it. SPN is a new form of non-fiction essay writing, and I am convinced that it is every bit as rigorous and as vigorous as other types of academically certified quantitative and qualitative research. In fact, if used well and wisely, SPN writing has the potential to enlarge, enrich, and deepen the more conventional meaning of academic scholarship. And when it does this, it speaks much more effectively to a variety of diverse student and non-student audiences.

What those of us in the academy need to realize is this: we currently live in an age of memoir writing. People love to tell their stories and to hear the stories of others. At this point in time, we in academia have not caught up to the world outside the ivy walls. For most university scholars, writing for a general public smacks of "mere journalism." Worse, if scholars strive to make their writing comprehensible to an audience beyond the university, then they run the risk of being charged with compromising the intellectual prestige of their disciplines. Moreover, say the critics, personal narrative writing doesn't win grants. Neither (as critics remind us) does it get faculty renewed contracts, tenure, promotion, or distinguished professorships.

There is a supreme irony here: in the pursuit of conventional rewards, many faculty lose the connection to their own personal histories. Consequently, a few faculty attempt to reconnect their professional and personal lives by waiting until much later in their careers to write more personally. This has been the case for me, as it took me 35 years to garner the courage to write my first personal book (Nash, 2002). I am relieved to say that neither the president, provost, nor dean at my university summarily dismissed me for my non-academic audacity. Neither did the "Objectivity Gods" strike me down with lightning bolts. In fact, in 2003 I was named the Official University of Vermont Scholar in the Social Sciences and Humanities.

Here is a somewhat disarming fact that all of us in higher education need to know: the printed and online books and articles that sell best nowadays are true-to-life personal narratives that appeal to a much larger public readership. Naomi Schaefer Riley (2011), an award-winning higher education journalist, reports that a book in the social sciences or humanities published by a university press is doing well if it sells a mere 300 copies, most of which are purchased by university libraries at inflated prices to cover the cost of printing. Likewise, a research-based article (according to economist Richard Vedder [2004], two million scholarly articles are published every year) in a refereed academic journal averages about a dozen readers at most.

The truth is that most faculty publish for one reason only: to avoid perishing—to secure tenure and promotion. I have heard a number of faculty throughout the country tell me that once these goals are reached, they are just not interested anymore in spending so much of their professional time obsessing about being published in obscure scholarly journals and in unreadable, technical books. Now they have the freedom to spend more time teaching, advising, and branching out in new directions in order to share their knowledge publicly. I believe that if university scholars could report their findings in accessible, engaging prose, and even tell a few personal stories along the way, they might get more feedback from readers. And reader response (whether positive or negative) can be a great motivator for a faculty member to continue writing and publishing. Otherwise, what's the use? Tenure and promotion are no longer a draw.

It is time for faculty to acknowledge that nothing is more appealing to readers (especially our students) than to experience an author's personal stories with meaning-making implications that can touch all their lives. No matter the age or stage, the personal or collective identity, everyone we know (whether professorial, professional, non-professional, or pre-professional; whether quarter-life, mid-life, or later-life) is dealing with meaning-making issues that will challenge them throughout their lifetimes. These are universal themes that are endemic to the human condition. They encompass understanding and implementing several life-sustaining hopes and dreams for the future and include the following: constructing a moral and ethical life-plan; choosing the right religion and spirituality to give strength and hope during difficult times; creating mutually beneficial core relationships that are lasting and loving; exploring intersecting identities that do not box or separate but, instead, result in making connections with others; knowing the difference between education and credentialism, as well as the difference between having a career and living a vocation; getting actively involved in civic engagement projects; learning how to deal with loss, pain, disappointment, and a sense of meaninglessness and purposelessness; and creating, as well as practicing, key strategies that will pay off in living a whole, healthy, joyful, and balanced life.

Whenever I teach my meaning-making class to undergraduates and graduate students, I receive the most compelling—and wise—writing from students of all ages who are working on these recursive life issues. I encourage all my students to dig deeply in order to tell their unvarnished personal stories of meaning-making—including their successes and failures, their joys and heartaches, and even their dreams realized and the nightmares that just won't stop coming. I have invited some of these students to publish their SPN essays in my books. Not coincidentally, many of my readers find these essays to be what connects them the most to the larger SPN themes I write about in my books. Why? Because nothing is a better theory-to-practice connective than candid, vulnerable stories lived by real, flesh-and-blood human beings who are trying to "write their lives as an act of personal witness." Nothing.

I believe that we academicians have reached an exciting time in the academy. The time has come—particularly when grant-seductive, STEM research methodologies are further disconnecting scholars from a more general audience—for each of the disciplines to look for the value in personal narrative writing. Actually, there is hope. Gerald Graff (2003), a leading literary scholar and former president of the Modern Language Association, lists the names of several highly respected scholars who are striving to combine the language of the personal vernacular with the technical terminology of their academic disciplines. I support this both/and approach to innovative scholarship. They are attempting to turn scholarly inaccessibility into public accessibility. Graff calls this mixture of writing styles a "bridge discourse" that could conceivably transform the meaning of scholarly writing in the academy. I prefer to call this "connection writing" because it holds the promise of connecting the "I" of the scholar to the "It" of the scholarship and, in turn, to the "minds and hearts" of all those in the community outside the university who might wish to engage with us.

ENCOURAGING MY STUDENTS TO BECOME SPN STORYTELLERS

I strongly believe that I am a better professor when I can speak in a language that is clear, down-to-earth, and non-technical. When I share my ideas with students, they really listen, and learn. I get their attention when I am willing to start from *inside of me* and then go *outside to them* in order to make real-world connections. In this sense, I am a communication-connector. This is also the way that I am learning how to write. When I tell personal stories and put specialized knowledge into a human context, my students learn how to do the same without fear of the usual professorial, "anti-intellectual" reprisals. My central belief is similar to that of MacArthur Genius Award Winner Ruth Behar, the anthropologist, who said: "Each of us needs to write our lives as an act of personal witness" (Behar, 1993). I want to be a scholar who writes from his heart as well as from his head. I want to bear true witness to myself in everything I do in higher education. Not only is this the right way of professing for me; through the years it has also brought out the best in my students. Or so they tell me.

What Behar means by "writing our lives as an act of personal witness" is to the point: scholars need to stop the "depersonalizing trend" in research that results in massive collections of so-called "objective data" regarding the "other," but nothing at all about the "self" who is collecting the data. A scholar who writes as an act of personal witness attempts to "desegregate the boundaries between the self and the other." Personal witness means to write "vulnerably." It is all about identifying, and acknowledging, the central role of the writer's personal experience in any type of scholarship. In Behar's words, "it requires a keen understanding of what aspects of the self are the most important filters through which one perceives the world and, more importantly, the topic being studied" (Behar, 1993, p. 33). Is there any better way than this to define the meaning of "public intellectual"? I don't know of any.

And, so, whenever my SPN classes meet for the first time, my co-teacher (Sydnee Viray) and I spend a good deal of time encouraging our students to write about their lives as an act of personal witness. This is a difficult task for most of them, as they have never written this way before in their courses. Some question the academic validity of this type of scholarly writing. Others wonder if they have anything important to say in writing about themselves that might be a useful take-away for readers. And still others question whether they even have it in them to express what we call a "narrative voice." Amid the doubts, therefore, we make it a point at the outset of the course to offer our students "five votes of SPN confidence" as they begin the journey of discovering, and using, their unique storyteller's voice:

1. Underneath all the protective layers of the self that you present to the world is a storyteller. As a storyteller, you will need to know how to develop colorful characters who engage readers at a number of levels. Readers need to care about the characters in your personal essay, and this includes caring about *you*, the author. You, after all, are the central character in your story. You are the primary conduit for all the meaning that your story will convey—whether you are a business major, a scientist, a mathematician, a religious studies scholar, or a historian.

2. You don't have to be some kind of *artistic* genius to write your story. Some writers are more visual than others. Some writers see images or word-pictures when they write. Some find it easy to create metaphors. You may be more of a literal thinker who relies on logic, analysis, and unpacking difficult ideas for readers. You may be a better essayist than you are a memoirist, poet, or fiction writer. Whatever your innate writing penchants, you will learn to go with your strengths as an SPN writer. The key is to tell your truth as honestly and clearly as you can, and if you are more of a "craft" person than an artist in your storytelling, be proud of this gift.

But don't forget to take some risks and venture into the realm of artistry, at least every now and then.

3. You can draw in your readers. This means that you will need to learn how to set the stage at the beginning of your story that will entice—even seduce—readers. You will need to know how to create "teaser-hooks" that will capture their attention. You will have to be aware of your "narrative arc" at all times. You will need to introduce your story's "plot line" somewhere at the beginning and refer back to it frequently during the course of your writing. This will be the best way to keep your readers on track. At the very least, your readers need to be willing to begin the journey with you. And, along the way, you will have to introduce conflicts, challenges, and other "high-stakes hooks" that will keep your readers' attention.

4. Every story you have lived in has reached some kind of a climax, or a series of climaxes. And some of these climaxes have also reached resolution. Keep this basic truth in front of you as you write: no reader begins a story looking to stop in the middle. The old Aristotelian adage that the best story is one with a beginning, middle, and end still holds true. All readers need the motivation to continue reading a story. Your story is no exception. And remember, too, that each and every story has its own natural *denouement*. The word is French, and it means "to untie knots." A denouement is the winding down of a story wherein all the narrative knots are untied for the reader (or at least most of them are). Readers need to feel some kind of satisfaction as they come to the end of your story. The implication for all of us as storytellers is not to avoid tying "knots" in our stories, but to be aware that too many "untied knots" leave readers in suspense and craving some kind of resolution. Remember this, however: writers can work hard to untie these knots while also realizing that our personal narrative stories never really end. They stop for a while, only to be continued later. Our stories go on and on until that inevitable day when our mortal bodies and minds die; even then, our stories live on in the people who mean the most to us and in the people who mean the most to them, ad infinitum.

5. You will eventually be able to identify those truths in your life that keep you together during the times when you feel as if you are coming apart. Ask yourself this question: What is really important to me at this particular time in my life? Remember that your storytelling in SPN writing is never an end in itself. Rather, it is a means to an end. You will learn, as time goes on, to reveal as much of your inner self as you choose in order to deliver the payload to your readers—the generalizable themes, truths, and insights. But while storytelling may not be its own end, it is the non-negotiable delivery system carrying the truths that may set readers free, at least momentarily, as they get immersed in your writing.

ADVICE TO AN EMAILER ON HOW TO BECOME
AN SPN PUBLIC INTELLECTUAL

The other day I received an email from a PhD candidate who will remain name-less. It is a good example of dozens like it that I receive monthly from all over the world. Here it is with a few minor additions and deletions:

Dear Dr. Nash,

I just finished reading your book, *Liberating Scholarly Writing*. I can't thank you enough for sharing your ideas and encouraging students to explore new forms of expression and still doing good scholarly work. By day, I am a high-tech executive, and by night a student who loves philosophy, leadership, social constructionism, and language. My "curse" is to try to blend my business-corporate self with the lover-of-ideas-and-learning self. It's a lonely place to occupy because my workplace colleagues and other executives see my PhD pursuit as a complete waste of time for someone running a global technology operation.

While I don't have all the answers, your book provided a clearing for me as well as access to think differently about the method and constructs of SPN writing and communication. I am hoping beyond hope that my doctoral program is progressive enough to support my pursuit of doing that which I find deeply meaningful. But what if it isn't? Anyway, thank you again for the wonderful written word. If you plan on visiting my city in 2013, drinks are on me. Perhaps we can talk about how I can become a writer who speaks not just to the academy, but also to people in the corporate business world, as well as to all of those folks who live outside of these two realities.

Sincerely yours,

xxxxxxxxxxxx

Here is the letter that I intend to send back to my online correspondent.

Dear Emailer,

How often have I heard from people like yourself who want to write as much on *your own* terms as on the academy's. While trained as a corporate executive, you also see yourself as a philosopher who would like to write for a larger public readership. You want to do Scholarly Personal Narrative writing that attempts to bridge the gaping chasm that often separates the academy from the world at large. You want to communicate your multi-dimensional intellectual interests to others in a jargon-free style so that they might be able to understand and apply your ideas. You seem to want desperately to be a border-crosser.

Perhaps you have already been told by higher-ups in your doctoral program department that in order to gain academic credibility, you will need to publish in refereed, scholarly journals and write books for prestigious university presses. An article in a so-called non-scholarly magazine with a readership of almost a million people will not do. Neither will a mono-graph count as serious scholarship, even one that is published by a professional association reaching tens of thousands of readers. Why not? Because this association does not send out manuscripts to external academic reviewers. In higher education, external reviewers are like gods. But professional associations keep all submitted manuscripts in-house for internal review. However, I, for one, know from firsthand experience that these internal reviews are much tougher, and more fair, than the conventional reviewers. For one, these internal reviewers have less to prove to their colleagues. For another, in-house reviewers are more interested in clarity, relevance, and, yes, marketability than they are in promoting the cause of clotted academic language.

I believe that, at this time, the best we can ever do in the academy is to report our scholarly findings in a format that also includes our intellectual stories, in our own words, and let the rewards fall where they may. If you might someday want to be a professor, I am convinced that somewhere there is a faculty evaluation committee, a department chair, and a dean who will find the wisdom in your personal stories to be both scholarly and tenurable. I know for sure, however, that you will be able to communicate your ideas more clearly and more inspiringly in your corporate workplace if you can come down to earth and speak the language of the "mere mortals" who work there. But please know not everyone in higher education believes that writing for a lay public is a debasement of genuine scholarship. You will find allies. Not all scholars consider SPN to be marginalized, "soft," non-rigorous writing.

In fact, some scholars themselves, usually later in their careers, strive to become journalists, media pundits, or online writers. Check out the work of such star public intellectuals as Richard Dawkins, Russell Jacoby, Martin Anderson, Gerald Graff, Irvin Yalom, Marian Wright Edelman, Anne Lamott, Annie Dillard, Jane Tompkins, Henry Louis Gates, Richard Rodriguez, and Cornel West, for starters. Some of these scholars have written memoirs, and all of them write frequently for a more general public audience. Many have written for one of my all-time favorite non-scholarly news publications, *The Chronicle of Higher Education*, which has a weekly readership of over one million, both in paper and online. In other words, their work actually gets read. It doesn't languish for years as a reference in a standardized curriculum vitae or get lost as a title in the depths of a departmental website.

I think it is highly revealing that at majestic Harvard University, Lawrence Buell, chair of the English Department, is in the process of building a community of public intellectuals like the writers I mention above. Here is what Buell (cited in Nash, 2004, pp. 149–150) said about his hiring practices:

> I want to blur the borders between the academy and the nonacademy…. We're not going to be fussy about the fact that [these hires] are not coming from an academic background. Value is value…. Border-crossing, whether between disciplines or crossing outside the academic tribe, is not only valuable for our students, it keeps the rest of us invigorated.

I can only say "Amen" to this.

So, dear emailer, my unsolicited advice to you might seem like the compromised position of someone thoroughly socialized by the academy, and it probably is. But I'll give it anyway.

If someday you decide to become a faculty member, try to be both a guerilla public intellectual *and* an out-university scholar, at least at the beginning of a faculty career. Don't get sucked into either/or thinking. There is no reason why you can't present your work in two dialects—university-speak and lay-talk. Do the research and scholarship that you need to do in order to benefit from the university's ever-traditional reward system. But also do the outside public communication you need in order to find your true satisfaction. Go ahead and translate your more academic work (for example, your dissertation) into an accessible idiom for laypersons—formally educated or otherwise. Write an autobiography, an op-ed piece, a blog, an article for an online newspaper or a bookstore magazine. Create an occasional communique for your business employees that is enjoyable to read, inspiring, and maybe even a little bit personal. You might be surprised at how motivational more of *you*, and a little less of the *information*, will be to your employees. As a number of writers have reminded us: the best leadership is "servant leadership," and this is relational, personal, collaborative, and hence inspiring. Isn't this type of leadership the best way to achieve results?

And maybe someday, when I am in your city, I will join you for a drink, but only on the condition that we can spend time sharing our personal as well as our professional stories with one another. This will be a wonderful way to practice making connections via storytelling communication.

Yours truly,
Robert J. Nash, Professor

CLOSING SPN WORDS FOR PROSPECTIVE PUBLIC INTELLECTUALS

What follows is a summary of Scholarly Personal Narrative writing principles that I believe would benefit those writers who yearn to communicate their truths beyond the confines of the academy to the larger world outside. I choose to present these principles briefly, in a bulleted format, because I have explained each one at length in four previous books I have written. And please remember: I make it a point to emphasize that the proper function of a scholar is to be able to speak compellingly to a number of diverse audiences. If a scholar's wisdom is confined only to the university library, in thousands of unread journals and books, then both the scholar and all those who are non-scholars are the losers. Even when these books and journals are available online, few people (if any) will read them if they are full of unreadable jargon, show-off, over-complicated mathematical equations, abstract ethereal arguments, and abstruse, in-house technical analysis.

After spending more than four and one-half decades in higher education, I'm sad that the observation of Page Smith rings true for me. Smith is an eminent historian, the author of more than 25 books, a former founding provost of the University of California, and a Harvard PhD.

> The vast majority of the so-called research turned out in the modern university is essentially worthless. It does not result in any measurable benefit to anything or anybody. It does not push back those omnipresent "frontiers of knowledge" so confidently evoked…. It is busywork on a vast, almost incomprehensible scale. (cited in Anderson, 1992, p. 99)

As I've expressed throughout this chapter, faculty research and scholarship do not have to be "worthless." If we can think of the scholarship we produce as being an exciting, rich mixture of me-search, re-search, and we-search, then we will be able to speak to larger and larger audiences, far beyond our tenure committees and fellow academic specialists. Our job as intellectuals is to teach, inform, and inspire others—as many others as possible. This will not happen, however, until we are ready to acknowledge that we exist for *them*; they don't exist for *us*. For example, without our students, there is no need for us, the faculty. Why can't we remember this in everything we do as professors? We need them more than they need us. We need the general public more than they need us.

So, in closing, here is a summary list of SPN writing principles that I give to all my undergraduate and graduate classes at the beginning of each semester and that I think are valuable to anyone considering making their writing more accesible and connecting to a broader world.

- First and foremost, SPN writing is not everyone's preference to write or to read, nor should it be seen as the One Compulsory Way of doing scholarly writing. At this point in time, it is more of a commonplace in the creative arts and writing seminars. But it is still an unwelcome stranger in most humanities courses, in professional schools, and in the social sciences and sciences. I wish that we scholars were more pluralistic in our academic undertakings. Why can't we encourage our students to try out all types of intellectual inquiry? Why is the "I" in a scholar's voice the one that must be censored in so many content areas?
- SPN writing starts with the "I" and proceeds outward to the "you" and the "they." The author's distinct and honest voice is key. The author's ideas are only as strong as the voice that delivers them. By the same token, absent the ideas, the personal voice can sometimes be seen as self-indulgent or overly confessional. The best way to deliver ideas to all people wherever they might live and work is to be honest, personal, empathic, and vulnerable. The choice of how vulnerable is up to you.
- SPN writing tells a good story and/or many good stories. We are all storytellers. We have to be in order to survive, to stay sane in a divided world, and to make allies, not enemies. If you want to engage the attention of all those around you, learn how to tell a story. Better still, learn how to evoke stories from others. Good SPN writing appeals to everyone—on campus,

to professors, administrators, students, and staff; and to most everyone off campus.

- SPN writing features a clear point of view, an organizing theme, and/or a coherent argument. It uses personal stories to deliver the message. It is no coincidence for SPN writers that the word *theme* is a combination of two words—*the* and *me*. Who I am is a collection of basic beliefs, meanings, and perspectives that are important to me. These change over time. But whatever these might be, they form the self, the mind, and the soul of the person. It is important to remember that the latter three entities will never show up in a CAT scan or an MRI. And yet without our "basic beliefs, meanings, and perspectives," there is no "me" there. The theme is always the main payload in SPN writing; the personal stories are a vehicle to deliver this payload.

- SPN strives for an ideal mix of particularity and generalizability, concreteness and abstractness, practice and theory. SPN writing has four major components. First, it starts with the identification of key *themes*. Second, it connects these themes to the writer's personal stories in order to exemplify and explicate the points being made. Third, it draws on relevant, pre-existing *research and scholarship* in order to ground and enrich the personal narrative. Finally, it ends up with *universalizable ideas and applications* that connect with all readers in some way.

- SPN does not present the author as some omniscient, third-person authority. The author's voice is personal, clear, fallible, and honest. It is also humble and open-ended. SPN writing shows some passion. It is not a detached, "objective" examination of a topic. It is a thoughtful, first-person attempt to make a point, or teach a lesson, by drawing on the author's own life experiences to provide context. It tries to help the reader to see the world a little differently, from the author's personal point of view.

- At times, SPN is more of an exercise in creative writing than it is writing to fit a particular research formula, rubric, or template. It takes personal risks. It begins with the self-confidence that the author has a personal story worth telling and a point worth making. But it always keeps front and center the interests of all the audiences who will read the work. Creative writing that takes chances and is imaginative is the most likely way to get others—especially those off campus—to spend time reading the author's words. It's time for all of us in higher education to realize that constructing a scholarly work does not have to be a dry, forbidding, or foreboding undertaking. It can be fun, engaging, and pleasing to write…and, perhaps even more important, for all others to read.

REFERENCES

Abbot, H.P. (2002). *The Cambridge introduction to narrative.* New York: Cambridge University Press.

Anderson, M. (1992). *Imposters in the temple: American intellectuals are destroying our universities and cheating our students of their future.* New York: Simon & Schuster.

Behar, R. (1993). *The vulnerable observer: Anthropology that breaks your heart.* Boston: Beacon Press.

Graff, G. (2003). *Clueless in academe: How schooling obscures the life of the mind.* New Haven, CT: Yale University Press.

Nash, R.J. (2002). *Spirituality, ethics, religion, and teaching: A professor's journey.* New York: Peter Lang.

Nash, R.J. (2004). *Liberating scholarly writing: The power of personal narrative.* New York: Teachers College Press.

Nash, R.J., & Bradley, D.L. (2011). *Me-search and re-search: A guide for writing scholarly personal narrative manuscripts.* Charlotte, NC: Information Age Publishing.

Nash, R.J., Johnson III, R.G., & Murray, M.C. (2012). *Teaching college students communication strategies for effective social justice advocacy.* New York: Peter Lang.

Nash, R.J., & Viray, S. (2013). *Our stories matter: Liberating the voices of marginalized students through scholarly personal narrative writing.* New York: Peter Lang.

Nash, R.J,. & Viray, S. (2014). *How stories heal: Writing our way to meaning and wholeness in the academy.* New York: Peter Lang.

Riley, N.S. (2011). *The faculty lounges: And other reasons why you won't get the college education you paid for.* Chicago: Ivan R. Dee.

Vedder, R. (2004). *Going broke by degree: Why college costs too much.* New York: AEI Press.

White, H. (1987). *The content of the form: Narrative discourse and historical representation.* Baltimore, MD: The Johns Hopkins University Press.

Engaging the Public Through Media and Web 2.0

CHAPTER FIVE

When a Public Intellectual Speaks Out But No One Hears Her, Does She Exist?

SUSAN OHANIAN

I just ordered a nifty T-shirt from the Academy of American Poets that features a line from Wallace Stevens's "Le Monocle de Mon Oncle" on the back—"I wish that I might be a thinking stone." And a scansion of that line across the front: ~/~/~/~/~/. Someone at the Academy of American Poets online store felt compelled to offer instruction, declaiming that there is "in fact room for disagreement about the scansion of this line." Prospective buyers of the T-shirt are told that although Stevens "probably heard it as five iambic feet...an alternative scansion is one iamb followed by a pyrrhic foot (two weak stresses) followed by two strong stresses (a spondee), followed by two iambs. It is also possible that all feet in the line are iambs except the third foot, though the word *might* most likely would have been italicized if that were the case."

Ohmigod. As Freud would have said, sometimes a T-shirt is just a T-shirt. Not wishing to be rude here, but I think this T-shirt scansion issue just might get to the core of my problem with the notion of "Public Intellectual in Education": Much educationese is neither intellectual nor anywhere near the public. I worry that such a concept even comes perilously close to being an oxymoron. I'm thinking here of "airline food," "Congressional ethics," "Department of Education intelligence." I nurture a long-held complaint about the insularity of academics— arguing about the content of Common Core standards while Rome burns and all that. But the other end of the spectrum is even more regrettable. I recently greeted with astonishment and then guffaws the existence of a rubric for assessing student

Tweets—copyrighted by an academic. Certainly, such a rubric—trying somehow to embrace popular culture—seems to blur the line between satire and stupidity. But it also forces the question: Just what could be a barometer of public intellectualism in education? Of course there has to be more than the weight of the footnotes one produces. I feel I can make somewhat snide remarks here because at the moment I have seven books in print with a leading educational publisher, and my most recent royalty check was $134.84. Total for seven books. Admittedly, the books have been around awhile, but is public intellectualism such a fickle entity that as my royalties shrink, indicating fewer readers, my claim to public intellectualism also diminishes? Is intellectualism tied to the dollar? You may shout "No!" but we are talking about *public* intellectualism, aren't we?

It's rather like the question of the tree falling in the forest. How can one claim to be *public* if there's no one listening?

YOU SAY POTATO...

For years I have been distressed by the silence of university scholars on the devastating impact of federal education policy. Or when they do talk they talk past each other. For example, scholars who write books about NCLB and Race to the Top rarely mention capitalism or the corporate domination of education policy. And scholars who write books about capitalism rarely mention NCLB and Race to the Top or the insidious influence of the U.S. Department of Education. Since scholars in neither camp offer any practical advice to teachers, by and large, their books sell only to the college classes required to buy them. Table 5.1 provides a rundown on the topics that interest these camps.

Table 5.1. Topics in Education Texts.

Selected Marxism Topics in Education Texts	Selected NCLB Topics in Education Texts
Capitalism	Academic Performance Index
Civil Society	Accountability
Commodities	Adequate Yearly Progress
Competition	Charter Schools
Corporations/Conglomerates	Civil Rights
Critical Pedagogy	Curriculum
Democracy	Demographics
Dialectal Contradictions	Data
Employment	English Language Learners

(*Continued*)

Table 5.1. (*Continued*).

Selected Marxism Topics in Education Texts	Selected NCLB Topics in Education Texts
Global Economy	Graduation Rates
Hegemony	History/Social Science
Human Beings	Low-Income Students
Justice	Mandatory Interventions
Knowledge	Proficiency Standards
Labor	Sanctions
Learning/Learners	Supplemental Educational Services
Marx	Testing
Poverty	Title 1
Praxis	U.S. Department of Education

"Oh, words, words, words, I'm so sick of words…. Is that all you blighters can do?"
—ELIZA DOOLITTLE, *MY FAIR LADY*.

Neither text mentions Dewey, Vygotsky, Dale's Cone of Experience, Campbell's Law, or Mary Budd Rowe's "wait-time." Nor does either text mention teacher professional organizations, or the House or Senate committees on education, or the Bill and Melinda Gates Foundation. One text barely mentions unions, doing so in such a fleeting reference as to be insignificant.

If I named the scholars listed in the indexes of these books, you could figure out who wrote the books because they mention their own work fulsomely, while excluding the work of Gerald Bracey, Richard Rothstein, David Berliner, and other scholars who have made a concerted effort to bring current education issues to public notice. Of course my own book, written with Kathy Emery, which lays out the corporate-politico foundations of NCLB in considerable detail, is rarely referenced in scholarly work because, not being university faculty, we aren't members of the guild (Emery & Ohanian, 2004). Saul Bellow once referred to *The New York Review of Each Other's Books*. That principle applies here. In *The Philosopher's Demise: Learning French*, Richard Watson (2003) observes that "If scholars talk to one another, all they have to talk about is their own work." Taleb (2010) calls this "The costs of specialization: architects build to impress other architects; models are thin to impress other models; academics write to impress other academics" (p. 48).

I would suggest that intellectualism is very dry toast if it isn't rooted in a concern for the public condition. A couch intellectual can publish on the postmodern semiotics of Freirean decision-making metrics, never leaving the couch except to appear before students a couple of times a week and read papers at AERA. I'll never forget the professor's response in a doctoral program when I challenged his characterization of Direct Instruction. "We have a lot of material to get through in time for the comps…lots of definitions. We don't have time for discussion." I wasn't a doctoral student; I was a teacher desperate to get three credits in reading theory before September, but I also wanted to learn something. The professor was prominent in the field, but ever since that episode, I couldn't read his papers without the bitter memory that in class he insisted on delivering a conveyor belt of definitions.

Surely, a public intellectual needs to have some sort of relationship with public life. I'm not insisting that this means marching on the steps of state capitols or even railing about the corporate oligarchy in letters to the editor, though I would ask *Why not?* Why are there so few voices from academia speaking out about Race to the Top? Why are so few talking about the Common Core Standards and how they lead directly to the national test that will destroy students and eat teacher professionalism alive?

Silence implies accommodation and feeds capitulation.

I hear those soulful stories from young academics: concern about rocking the boat before they have tenure; being swamped by student papers and committee obligations; worry about disrupting the money flow from the U.S. Department of Education, and increasingly, the Bill and Melinda Gates Foundation, for research grants. I don't quite see how university folk hoping to travel with public intellectual passports can continue to avoid the big problems of our time, but I worry that, increasingly, big money defines the problems. Take a look at a few grants from the Bill and Melinda Gates Foundation that may be small potatoes when one considers the Gates gift of $25,041,228 to the National Governors or the $90 million "Intensive Partnership Grant" to the Memphis City Schools Board of Commissioners. But think about the effect of the grants like the ones below on individual educators as possible public intellectuals.

American Educational Research Association
Date: May 2013
Purpose: to fund the selection and support of nine doctoral scholars who will conduct research in the area of teaching effectiveness using the Measures of Effective Teaching longitudinal database
Amount: $250,000

University of Southern California
Date: November 2012
Purpose: to understand how measures of effective teaching can accelerate skills development for teaching candidates enrolled in USC Rossier School of Education's Masters of Arts in Teaching program
Amount: $110,000

Stanford University
Date: June 2012

Purpose: to support development of a chapter about Quality Science Teaching instrument for the edited volume of the Measures of Effective Teaching project
Amount: $30,000

Harvard University
Date: June 2012
Purpose: to support development of a chapter about the relationship of student to teacher survey responses for the edited volume of the Measures of Effective Teaching project
Amount: $30,000

The Rand Corporation also received $30,000 for a chapter in that book; Educational Testing Service received $45,000 "to support development"; the University of Texas $50,000; the University of Virginia $49,864. And so on and so on. Those of us contributing essays to the volume you hold in your hands will consider ourselves lucky to receive a free copy of the book from the publisher.

TEACHING AND THINKING AT THE SAME TIME

I know firsthand why there are so few public intellectuals among schoolteachers. For my first 5 years of teaching I buried myself in my own classroom. After that, my main effort at looking beyond my own classroom was to produce a monthly union newsletter. My claim to fame there is that my public deconstruction of administrative memos cut the number of said memos appearing in teacher mailboxes by 77%. Over a decade, I bullied *New York Teacher* into publishing book reviews and published some small pieces in a few national publications. When the editor of *Learning* magazine phoned and asked me for a cover story on classroom discipline, he was both astounded and dismayed when I said such a big topic would take me about 6 months. I explained, "I can't teach and write at the same time. Teaching fills my days and getting ready to teach fills my nights." When he phoned back, offering me the job as the magazine's first staff writer, I accepted. In those days, people working in classrooms didn't get published, and I saw this as a great opportunity to go public in a big way and speak for The Teacher.

I'd never made any pretense of being an intellectual, but I saw the writing job as an opportunity to let teachers know they weren't alone. Certainly, nobody who's not in the classroom day after day, year after year, has a clue how lonely that space is. Surrounded by upward of 25 students (or 150 and upward at the secondary level) with individual and often critical needs, the teacher is all by herself.

From those days as staff writer to my current position for more than 12 years as self-appointed Queen of Website Resistance, I've always felt I'm carrying the banner for my many unmet colleagues out there, doing their jobs as best they can (which I know from traveling the country and visiting classrooms in 28 states is pretty darn good). Some teachers are breathtakingly intellectual; others worry about what to do on Monday. Most are tough, resilient, caring, dedicated—and smart. None gets more than a modicum of help from anybody. These days the corporate-politicos scream about the public's right to know what an excellent teacher looks like. I'd say that after chasing hamsters, interrogating boys about the toilet paper wads on the lavatory ceiling, and listening to "I'm telling" all day, as well as leading children toward countless encounters with words that enrich their lives, the excellent teacher probably looks tired.

I'd rate an excellent teacher pretty much the same way I'd rate an excellent parent. Let me count the ways. One teacher cries when her students walk out the door on the last day of school without looking back. Another puts an 8-year-old's desk in the dumpster when he lollygags in the lavatory. We must ignore Bill Gates's money and rid ourselves of the notion that the model of an ideal teacher exists. Excellence is varied: sometimes subtle, other times noisy. Excellence is often opinionated, stubborn, and intractable. Excellence is rarely docile and often breaks the rules. In writing about parenthood, Michael Chabon (2009) describes the "monumental open-endedness of the job, with its infinite number of infinitely small pieces...."

But Bill Gates, in love with his Grand Plan, doesn't understand small, complex pieces. Bill thinks that by videotaping classrooms, his "experts" can collect all the relevant data about teacher job performance. I say, "A whole lot depends on who's watching the video." My experience is that it takes a very knowledgeable eye to see what's really happening in the "infinite number of infinitely small pieces."

I remember when my department chair, hired because she was a manager, not because she knew a thing about teaching, decided to do an official observation of my 7th–8th-grade classroom. Students were engaged in half a dozen separate activities. A few were working in pairs or small groups. Most worked individually. One slept. I could have provided pedagogical context for every one—even the sleeper. I was inordinately pleased to have a witness to such a good day. But after 20 minutes, my boss couldn't take it anymore. She left, saying she'd come back when I was teaching a lesson. These days, we have hordes of video analyzers armed with checklists sent in from distant empires, not to bear witness but to record data—pursuing not an intellectual, or even a thoughtful, endeavor.

One of my jobs as staff writer was to develop what came to be called "Difficult Person," a short, snappy account of how a teacher uses her ability, her wisdom, her doggedness to solve people problems. Most often, the difficult persons were students, but they could also be another teacher, a parent, or a principal. I like telling stories, and I had plenty of classroom incidents on which to draw, but one day I complained to the editor-in-chief that in the real world lots of classroom dilemmas aren't resolved; no neat-and-tidy solutions appear. The editor-in-chief wouldn't hear of it. She stated that we were a magazine that offered solutions, not stalemates. What people putting out the magazine couldn't grasp is that a teacher is a person who fails every day. Every day. She can hope to succeed every day, too, but the failures gnaw and grind away. I knew it then and I know it now. The "best and the brightest" are not the people we need in our schools. We need the savvy, rock steady, dependable, loving, forgiving people who have an enormous capacity for wait time and the psychological equilibrium to be able to enter the classroom every day not holding a grudge about what happened the day before—people who have the capacity to live with mistakes.

But the corporate claim is insistent: Every problem has a solution. After all, those folks at Nabisco offer a website where you can "learn everything you want about America's Favorite Cookie!" And the Bill and Melinda Gates Foundation is bent on something similar. Paying off everybody from the National Governors Association, the PTA, and AERA, and the National Council of Teachers of English to ASCD, Stanford, Harvard, and NBC's *Education Nation* (and multitudes of others), they proclaim, "Let us tell you everything you need to know about America's teachers!"

GOING PUBLIC, WHO GETS QUOTED

My research for *Extra!* was an opportunity to prove—or disprove—the commonly held academic complaint that despite all the conversation about Race to the Top (RTTT), there is little serious questioning of this radical federal deformation and displacement of what should be local school policy. So I started counting press citations. The results are shocking, confirming our worst fears—and then some. I read some 700 newspaper articles on the subject of RTTT and the Common Core standards published between mid-May 2009 and mid-July 2010. With one exception, I eliminated citations from state education officials, union officials, and politicos. This left me with 152 outside experts cited in 414 articles. Just 23 "experts" were quoted five or more times. Of these, 15 have connections with institutions receiving funding from the Bill and Melinda Gates Foundation and 13 with institutions making strong advocacy for charter schools. The way the press identifies experts conceals their allegiances from the reader, something that is very concerning. For example, Chester Finn, Mike Petrilli, and Andy Smarick at the pro-standards Thomas B. Fordham Institute were cited 49 times. *Education Week* wants you to know that Smarick is a "prolific writer on Race to the Top," not seeing the need to provide a more telling identifier here than "prolific." When citing Finn (president of the Fordham Institute), Sam Dillon and Tamar Lewin at *The New York Times* identify him simply as "president of an education research group in Washington." In another article, Dillon identifies him as "writer of an influential education blog." Nobody mentions that Finn is also a fellow at the hyper-conservative Hoover Institution, or that he received the Rotten Apple award from the late Gerald Bracey, a noted scholar, more than once. These days, when talking of education reform, what we really need are reporters who follow the money.

Education Week quoted Fordham Institute people in three articles in the same issue. No matter what one's opinion is of the Thomas B. Fordham Institute, something's clearly amiss when an outfit receiving big money from the Bill and Melinda Gates Foundation is quoted 49 times (with only one reference to this Gates money) and David Berliner and Richard Rothstein not once. I would note that Rothstein, a research associate for the Economic Policy Institute in Washington, D.C., and author of several books, including *Grading Education: Getting Accountability Right*, has called the Obama administration's approach to education, which, among other things, would convert some Title I funding to competitive grants, nothing short of "tragic." Wouldn't you think an alert press would ask him about this? In April 2010, the Economic Policy Institute published Rothstein and William Peterson's *Let's Do the Numbers: Department of Education's "Race to the Top" Program Offers Only a Muddled Path to the Finish Line* (2010), a source never mentioned in the 700+ press articles on Race to the Top in this very time period. For years, Rothstein has been reminding people that no matter how many fourth graders pass the test, their scores won't raise the minimum wage. The education press seems incapable of hearing this message—and certainly does not share it with the public. They'd rather call on the Fordham Institute.

And why would the press shut out David Berliner, co-author of the acclaimed *Manufactured Crisis: Myths, Fraud, and the Attack on America's Public Schools* (Berliner & Biddle, 1996) and *Collateral Damage: How High-Stakes Testing Corrupts America's Schools* (Nichols & Berliner, 2007) while citing Joe Williams and his cohort Charles Barone at the Democrats for Education Reform 40 times? We can ask why the press is more comfortable talking with leaders of a political action committee (PAC) tied to hedge funds than with an acclaimed scholar very familiar with the nitty gritty of how schools work.

Here are two press citations among the 700+ that are uniquely noteworthy for informing the public. "The Gates program and the Arne Duncan program are pretty much the same program," Nancy C. Detert, chair of the Education Committee in the Florida Senate, told *The New York Times* (October 28, 2009). Mike Petrilli, vice president of the Thomas B. Fordham Institute, agrees, telling the *Puget Sound Business Journal* (May 15, 2009), "It is not unfair to say that the Gates Foundation's agenda has become the country's agenda in education."

The *Business Journal* noted that as of that date, the Fordham Institute itself had received nearly $3 million in Gates Foundation grants.

The press often goes to Gene Wilhoit for an expert opinion. Wilhoit is executive director of the nonprofit Council of Chief State School Officers. As of December 2013, his group and the National Governors Association Center for Best Practices, its partner in spearheading the drive for the Common Core standards, have received $108,572,740 from the Gates Foundation. In *Bloomberg Businessweek*, Daniel Golden revealed the man behind the curtain, pointing out that the Bill and Melinda Gates Foundation "bankrolled the development of the common curriculum standards." Golden writes: "Today, the Gates Foundation and Education Secretary Duncan move in apparent lockstep" on an agenda Golden calls "an intellectual cousin of the Bush administration's 2002 No Child Left Behind law" (Golden, 2010). Golden also pointed to the tidy sum that the Thomas B. Fordham Institute gave to provide analysis of the Common Core.

Of the 152 experts cited in the articles under review, 24 are associated with universities, but you won't find anybody elucidating pedagogy or practice here— because the press calls on university economists and statisticians. With other press favorites, it's up to the reader to figure out what the agenda might be when the press quotes people associated with groups such as the New America Foundation, New Schools Venture Fund, New Leaders for New Schools, Mass Insight, and on and on—without a hint about what their pro-market agenda might mean for public education.

Can one be a public intellectual if one's voice never reaches the public? Case in point: the National Council of Teachers of English (NCTE) set up an office in Washington, D.C., in an attempt to make its voice heard, to get a seat at the corporate political table. NCTE was not cited in a single one of the 700+ articles, nor was the National Council of Teachers of Mathematics. The International Reading Association was briefly cited twice.

Here is a list of the experts quoted in the press who received five or more citations and the minimalist identification provided by the press. A public that wanted to be informed would have to do considerable research. For example, the Center for Education Reform is a strident advocate for charter schools and school choice, and Democrats for Education Reform is a Political Action Committee (PAC) supported largely by hedge fund managers favoring charter schools, merit pay tied to test scores, high-stakes testing, school choice (including vouchers and tuition tax credits, in some cases), mayoral control, and alternative teacher preparation programs. An identifier such as "high-stakes testing advocate" provides quite different information from the usual press descriptor "director of federal policy." The more you know about the affiliations and agendas of these "experts," the more incensed you will be by the press "identifiers" provided below.

- Jeanne Allen, president of the Center for Education Reform
- Charles Barone, director of federal policy, Democrats for Education Reform
- Michael Cohen, president of Achieve Inc.
- Timothy Daly, president of the New Teacher Project
- Chester Finn, president of Thomas B. Fordham Institute
- Eric Hanushek, of Hoover Institution
- Fred M. Hess, of American Enterprise Institute
- E.D. Hirsch, founder of Core Knowledge
- Caroline Hoxby, Stanford University economist
- Jack Jennings. President of Center on Education Policy
- Dane Linn, education division director, National Governors Association
- McKinsey and Company
- Mike Petrilli, with the Thomas B. Fordham Institute
- Diane Ravitch, education historian
- Andrew Rotherham, co-founder Education Sector; co-founder Bellwether Education
- Jon Schnur, co-founder New Leaders for New Schools
- Andy Smarick, with Thomas B. Fordham Institute and American Enterprise Institute
- Kate Walsh, president of National Council on Teacher Quality
- Joanne Weiss, Race to the Top director
- Grover "Russ" Whitehurst, director of the Brown Center on Education Policy and a senior fellow at the Brookings Institution
- Gene Wilhoit, executive director of Council of Chief State School Officers
- Amy Wilkins, vice president of government affairs and communications at Education Trust
- Joe Williams, executive director, Democrats for Education Reform

I'd like evidence that more than two of these experts on public education policy have ever set foot in a public school—or talked to a public school teacher. Diane Ravitch, cited six times, is probably the one person on this list who qualifies as an education intellectual, and with her 2010 barnstorming of the country in opposition to Race to the Top, "Waiting for Superman," and allied concerns, she also qualifies as *public*. I was cited three times in these articles, identified each time as "blogger." Curious that there was no mention of the fact I taught for 20 years and have written 25 books, I now watch press citations more carefully, wondering why straight news articles so rarely mention that experts cited have written any books.

During the period under scrutiny, there were a number of feature stories on Diane Ravitch's famous change of mind, resulting in *The Death and Life of the Great American School System: How Testing and Choice Are Undermining Education* (2010). But no Ravitch cites in the 700+ articles under discussion mention that she's written numerous books. This is an odd exhibit of anti-intellectualism on the part of our national press. After all, as Louis Menand notes in *The New Yorker* (November 22, 2010), "A blog is a means of sharing your pet peeves and off-the-cuff theories of everything with the entire planet. To this point in the history of civilization, that is not what a book is. In a book, normally, one's eye is on a somewhat farther horizon." The press, from *The New York Times* to the *Anchorage Daily News*, shuns that farther horizon when identifying people whom they call on to explain what's happening in public education.

Of course, one can't take for granted these days that people at what used to be known as institutions of higher learning have much interest in intellectualism, public or otherwise. Here's college executive Michael Crow's view: "We use the word 'academic entrepreneurs.' We are expanding what it means to be a knowledge enterprise. We use knowledge as a form of venture capital." They might as well say knowledge as predatory cannibalism. Executive vice provost at Columbia University at the time, Crow became president of Arizona State University 5 months later (Blumenstyk, 2001, p. A29). Knowledge as a form of venture capital seems very much in line with the policy of the Obama/Duncan team—and with who gets quoted in the press as education expert. Nine years later, the *Chronicle* cited Crow as "the kind of college leader that defines institutional success: having a balance of vision, and sometimes aggressive self-confidence." An irate reader described this as college branding that "reeks of the same type of cultural necrosis that permeates reality shows" (Carlson, 2010).

HOW TO GO FROM EXPERT TO IGNOMINY IN 24 HOURS

12/9, 6:45 p.m. From *The New York Times* **to Susan Ohanian:** We are putting together a discussion on our online opinion forum, Room for Debate (http://www.nytimes.com/roomfordebate), about stress among high school students. These discussions are meant to be mini op-eds (about 300 words by a variety of experts addressing a specific question. Here's the question: *A new documentary, "Race to Nowhere," is hitting a nerve among parents across the country who are worried about the levels of stress that their school-age children are experiencing* [Gabriel, 2010]. *What can schools—and parents—do to turn down the heat?*

I sent them 307 words. After a back-and-forth for much of the day, we resolved all issues except for one sentence in what *The New York Times* refers to as the penultimate paragraph. I call it "The Thomas Friedman Problem."

2/10, 7:53 a.m. From Susan to *The New York Times*: 307 words
Original Text Excerpt: Parents and teachers must fight for childhood. Say "No!" to Barack Obama, to Thomas Friedman, to Ben Bernanke, to Oprah, and to everybody else who mouths nonsense about educating workers for the global economy, trying to put the blame for our economic woes on the backs of schoolchildren.

1:35 p.m., *New York Times* **Edit:** Parents and teachers must fight for childhood. Say "No!" to everybody who mouths this nonsense about educating workers for the global economy, trying to put the blame for our economic woes on the backs of schoolchildren.

2:33 p.m., Susan to *The New York Times*: Why has this paragraph been stripped of content? Saying "everybody" doesn't hold anyone responsible. Is one not allowed to criticize the influential people who mouth the global economy nonsense? I want the original paragraph back.

3:49 p.m., *The New York Times* **to Susan:** Regarding your penultimate paragraph, our feeling is that it seems odd to blame such a large audience—celebrities, etc.—when the fault lies with the policymakers and education experts, so hopefully you're okay with that tweak, which goes back to most of your original wording.
New York Times **Edit:** Parents and teachers must fight for childhood. Say "No!" to political leaders and education policy experts who mouth this nonsense about educating workers for the global economy, trying to put the blame for our economic woes on the backs of schoolchildren.

7:17 p.m., Susan to *The New York Times*: I wrote a book called *Why Is Corporate America Bashing Our Public Schools?* detailing why the fault most definitely does NOT lie with education experts. The current education policy [NCLB] was planned by the Business Roundtable; with help from politicos like Gov. Bill Clinton and IBM chief Lou Gerstner. Obama has come late to the party, but he's there. Thomas Friedman, for one, frequently orates about our economy depending on school children taking college prep curriculum. His words are quoted by CEOs and politicos. I'm willing to take out Oprah, though every teacher would know why her name is there.

That was the end of the exchange. I did not hear from anyone at *The New York Times* again. Writing on language in the *New York Times Magazine*, Ben Zimmer says it is unlikely that Mark Twain ever made this remark often attributed to him: "Only kings, presidents, editors, and people with tapeworms have the right to use the editorial 'we'" (2010). Regardless, I do note the editorial "we" ("our feeling") tossed in my direction.

Over the course of the edits, *The New York Times* removed my suggestion that the state of Vermont should apologize to the high school student, and I okayed it. When they substituted "truck drivers" for "yurt builders," I pointed out that in that sentence yurt builders represent a particular group of people who don't want to be standardized, but I agreed to the change. When I stood firm on laying blame for student anxiety at the feet of Obama, Friedman, and Bernanke (offering to remove Oprah as a gesture of compromise), suddenly *The New York Times* reinstated the state of Vermont apology and the yurt builders. I interpreted this as an attempt to get me on board regarding Obama, Friedman, and Bernanke. "Give her back the yurt builders, so she'll shut up about Friedman!"

Although *The New York Times* initially addressed me as an expert, in the end neither my research nor my opinion counted for a hill of beans. Five people contributed to Room for Debate on December 12, 2010, blaming student stress on a variety of things including AP classes, homework, too many after-school activities. Nobody blames Thomas Friedman. I know that not one reader in 1,000 will understand the Friedman sentence. And of those who do understand it, not one in 10,000 will think I was right to destroy my chances of getting into *The New York Times* by insisting on it. After all, doesn't getting our words into *The New York Times* validate us as genuinely important? The problem is that I happen to believe that op-eds should increase public understanding, not just preach to the orthodoxy of those who already agree. I think people should puzzle over why Friedman's name is there. I hope that a few would even ask some questions.

Most will think *The New York Times* won. Maybe so, but I think their victory would have been bigger had I gone along with the deal to remove that sentence. And since I posted this exchange on my website, I have received an outpouring of support from teachers and parents, people I've never met, people grateful that I stood stubbornly for that sentence.

HOW TO GET INTELLECTUAL FAST

Dismayed by my failure to rouse the public beyond readers of my website, perhaps it's understandable that I'd be attracted to a little book by Peter Archer: *The Quotable Intellectual* (2010). This book includes quips by two Allens, Fred and Woody; two Marxes, Groucho and Karl; Maya Angelou, Yassir Arafat, Buddha, Erma Bombeck, Albert Camus, Coco Chanel, Zsa Zsa Gabor, Hermann Goering, Søren Kierkegaard, Dean Koontz, Alfred North Whitehead, Tammy Wynette, Zeno, Frank Zappa, and Dave Barry. It's mindboggling to scan the index and see these people sitting next to each other—as intellectuals. I guess nobody would quarrel that dead Greeks are intellectuals, but Frank Zappa?

The publisher's blurb explains: "Have you ever wanted to be an intellectual, without all that tedious work of getting an advanced college degree? Here's your shortcut to the world of the well read. Just open this collection of 1,417 quotations from the mouths of the wildly famous to the painfully obscure, and *voila!*—instant erudition." I'm still not sure how quoting Zsa Zsa Gabor or Dean Koontz convinces anyone you're an intellectual, but scanning the index made me realize how few people "qualify." Dave Barry is a lot of fun, but is he intellectual enough to rate seven citations? And yet, reading Saul Bellow's collected letters may give one pause about dismissing people out of hand. After dinner with Marilyn Monroe, Bellow wrote to his publisher: "Surrounded by thousands, she conducts herself like a philosopher" (Bellow, 2010, p. x). He didn't explain what he meant.

Call me old-fashioned, but Gore Vidal was my idea of a public intellectual: general all-around man of letters, sometime political activist, penultimate impaler of pomposity. Vidal's essays are as timely today as they were 30 years ago. Reviewing a collection of Vidal's essays, Jonathan Rabin (2008) speaks of "a first-class mind in action, at once severely rational, rich in personal memories, alarmingly well-read, and almost indecently prone to fits of impious laughter," also noting Vidal's "ever-growing fury with those who...meekly connive at the deterioration of the US into a brutal and self-serving corporate oligarchy." If those in academia aspiring to public intellectualism wanted to learn from Vidal, a good place to start would be "fits of impious laughter."

REFERENCES

Archer, P. (2010). *The quotable intellectual.* Avon, MA: Adams Media.

Bellow, S. (2010). *Saul Bellow letters* (B. Taylor, Ed.). Peabody, MA: Viking Adult.

Berliner, D.C., & Biddle, B.J. (1996). *The manufactured crisis: Myths, fraud, and the attack on America's public schools.* Reading, MA: Addison Wesley.

Blumenstyk, G. (2001, February 9). Knowledge is a form of venture capital for a top Columbia administrator. *Chronicle of Higher Education,* p. A29.

Carlson, S. (2010, November 14). How to build a perception of greatness. *Chronicle of Higher Education.* Retrieved from http://chronicle.com/article/How-to-Build-the-Perception-of/ 125374/?sid=at&utm_source=at&utm_medium=en

Chabon, M. (2009, July 16). Manhood for amateurs: The wilderness of childhood. *New York Review of Books.* Retrieved from http://www.nybooks.com/articles/archives/2009/jul/16/ manhood-for-amateurs-the-wilderness-of-childhood/

Emery, K., & Ohanian, S. (2004). *Why is corporate America bashing our public schools?* Portsmouth, NH: Heinemann.

Gabriel, T. (2010, December 9). Parents embrace documentary on pressures of school. *The New York Times,* p. 23A.

Golden, D. (2010, July 15). Bill Gates' school crusade: The Microsoft founder's foundation is betting billions that a business approach can work wonders in the classroom. *Business Week.* Retrieved from http://www.businessweek.com/magazine/content/10_30/b4188058281758. htm

Nichols, S.L., & Berliner, D.C. (2007). *Collateral damage: How high-stakes testing corrupts America's schools.* Cambridge, MA: Harvard Education Press.

Peterson, W., & Rothstein, R. (2010). *Let's do the numbers: Department of Education's "Race to the Top" program offers only a muddled path to the finish line.* Washington, DC: Economic Policy Institute. Retrieved from http://epi.3cdn.net/4835aafd6e80385004_5nm6bn6id.pdf

Rabin, J. (2008, December 18). The prodigious pessimist. *New York Review of Books.* Retrieved from http://www.nybooks.com/articles/archives/2008/dec/18/the-prodigious-pessimist/

Ravitch, D. (2010). *The death and life of the great American school system: How testing and choice are undermining education.* New York: Basic Books.

Room for Debate. (2010, December 12). Stress and the high school student. *The New York Times.* Retrieved from http://www.nytimes.com/roomfordebate/2010/12/12/stress-and-the-high-school-student

Rothstein, R. (2008). *Grading education: Getting accountability right.* New York: Teachers College Press & Economic Policy Institute.

Taleb, N.N. (2010). *The black swan: The story of the highly improbable* (2nd ed.). New York: Random House.

Watson, R. (2003). *The philosopher's demise: Learning French.* Boston, MA: David R. Godine.

Zimmer, B. (2010, October 13). On language: Truthiness. Retrieved from http://www.nytimes.com/2010/10/17/magazine/17FOB-onlanguage-t.html

CHAPTER SIX

The Naked Seminar

Blogging as Public Education Outside the Classroom

SHERMAN DORN

Academics are supposed to be public intellectuals, Russell Jacoby tells us—or rather complains that professors are among the "anonymous souls, who may be competent, and more than competent, but who do not enrich public life."[1] More than a half-century after the expansion of both higher education institutions in the United States and the doctorally educated professoriate, the role of academics in public debate is precarious. There has never been a golden age of academic influence in the United States, but there is an irony in the relative failure of professors to engage the general public over the last third of a century, when the proportion of young adults with college degrees has been higher than at any previous point in American history. We reach students in classes, but do we reach graduates or those who never enroll in college?

The Internet has made such outreach much easier, providing a number of tools for faculty to write about ideas that are important to them. Among the most prominent are static web resources, podcasting, video sites (such as YouTube channels), and blogs. Since the mid-1990s, more academics have created websites, not only relying on institutional resources available to them but also reserving domain names for use as private venues for their writing and the distribution of ideas. Groups of academics have created networks to spread ideas not only among academic peers but also to anyone with an interest in specific issues. For example, in the mid-1990s, academics who had created email journals in a number of fields started shifting these progenitors to open-access journals, accelerating web-based publication available to the entire world and not just the subscribers to email lists. Also in the mid-1990s, the University of Michigan MATRIX humanities center became the facilitating point for H-Net, a collection of email distribution lists that fostered discussion among specific topics (the majority tied to fields of history). In 1996, the History News Service began an organized effort to edit and distribute historians' opinion pieces to newspaper op-ed editors.

The past decade has seen an acceleration in the development of such tools. The evolution of podcasting has allowed the distribution of radio shows and their equivalent beyond limited syndication of most public-interest radio. For example, the Virginia Foundation for the Humanities sponsored *Backstory Radio*, an hour-long history radio show that is available as a podcast to listeners who are not in range of the 100-plus stations that broadcast it or cannot listen to it at broadcast time; now it has become a weekly radio show. Video distribution services such as YouTube and iTunes have allowed associate anthropology professor Michael Wesch to co-produce and distribute a video with a 2007 class at Kansas State University and for astrophysicist Walter Lewin to lecture about physics to audiences far from his MIT campus.[2] The more recent development of eBook publishing has allowed faculty such as economist Tyler Cowen to produce and sell writing faster than is usually possible through university or commercial presses, as well as distribute writing free of charge through websites. And eBook production has allowed university presses to reach a broader audience and create an additional stream of revenue beyond academic library purchases.

In this context, blogging serves as one of many Internet tools for faculty when they wish to act as public intellectuals. The technical ease of publishing a blog entry eliminates a significant source of friction in writing for the public. With a self-published blog, there is no gatekeeper and a much-reduced need for technical expertise in the specifics of developing and maintaining a website. The past 10 years have seen the development of a range of platforms for blogging, and many who have written blogs over this period have used several services and platforms. As a new assistant professor in 1996, I used my college's webserver to create a limited set of pages that I hand-coded as HTML, and I updated those pages for a decade. In 2000 and 2001, a friend began exploring the earliest wave of social media, including *LiveJournal,* and based on her enthusiasm, I created an account on *LiveJournal* in early 2001 for blog entries related to my professional life.[3] As with many professionals who experimented with blogging early in the decade, I did not have a set goal for blogging other than setting down some experiences—in my case, an assistant professor a few months away from applying for tenure. The early entries in my professional blog are best described as slice-of-life pieces on idiosyncratic topics in academe: research projects, the process of writing, grading loads, work-life balance, computer woes, observations about the community, lack of sleep, inspirational moments, and thoughtful challenges by students.

Four years later, I found my blog becoming a significant opportunity for discussing threats to academic freedom in Florida and around the world. Two events precipitated this change in my blog: legislation threatening academic freedom that a conservative state legislator introduced in the Spring 2005 legislative session in Florida, and public attacks on then-Professor Ward Churchill of the University of Colorado. In 2004–2005, the Florida legislature became one of the key flashpoints as right-wing writer David Horowitz launched a campaign attacking faculty around the country. At the time, Horowitz had been for two decades a 1960s leftist radical-turned-conservative writer, having written several books and raised funds for the Center for the Study of Popular Culture, which he founded and which was the publisher of two conservative magazines, first *Heterodoxy* and later *Front Page Magazine*. Horowitz's center was in the middle of launching several cultural politics campaigns in the decade after the September 11, 2001, attacks, such as "Discover the Networks" and "JihadWatch," the first of which was dedicated to the argument that a significant number of college and university faculty in the United States were politically disloyal in some way.[4]

In 2003, David Horowitz began pushing for legislation that would have provided government oversight and ideological scrutiny of classroom teaching. He developed what became known as the "Academic Bill of Rights," and Rep. Jack Kingston introduced it as a concurrent resolution in November 2003.[5] Kingston's resolution was a sense-of-Congress statement that states should adopt a "bill of rights" for students. Horowitz's proposed bill was first introduced as a potential statute in a state legislature in Colorado in 2003–2004, and most formulations combined vague statements about freedom of conscience with proposed mechanisms that were intrusive and threatened academic freedom. For example, the bill introduced in Florida during the 2005 regular legislative session would have provided a cause of action (or a mechanism for a lawsuit) for students who were unhappy with the academic judgments made by faculty in presenting material in the classroom.[6]

In 2004, a national meeting of conservative state legislators helped connect Horowitz with state-level politicians by endorsing his proposed Academic Bill of Rights at its spring meeting in late April.[7] Earlier that spring, in March, the Georgia State Senate had approved a version of the bill, and in Horowitz's home state of California, Senator Bill Morrow introduced the bill in February 2004, though Morrow's bill only attracted one vote in committee.[8] The 2004 endorsement by the American Legislative Exchange Council (ALEC) provided model legislative language for conservative lawmakers around the country, and Horowitz and his center expended considerable time publicizing the bill in 2004, 2005, and 2006. In several states, Horowitz found a much friendlier audience than California, especially in Pennsylvania and Florida. When Rep. Dennis Baxley (Ocala) introduced a bill in Florida and it started moving quickly through the lower chamber, it attracted attention, and I used my blog in the spring of 2005 to track the legislation and discussion of it.[9]

Concurrent with Horowitz's attacks on academic freedom was the developing controversy and later investigation of University of Colorado Prof. Ward Churchill. At the time, Churchill was a full professor and chair of the Department of Ethnic Studies and was scheduled to speak at Hamilton College on February 3, 2005. In the week before the scheduled speech at the upstate New York college, a *New York Post* reporter publicized the speech.[10] Fox News talk-show host Bill O'Reilly called the appearance outrageous, in large part because of an article Churchill had written in late 2001 calling the September 11, 2001, attack on the World Trade Center "a few more chickens...[coming home] to roost in a very big way" and referring to the World Trade Center functionaries as a "perpetrator population," or "little Eichmanns," suggesting culpability on the part of either Western capitalism or (for many readers) those who died in the attacks.[11] In response to threats called into the college, Hamilton's president cancelled the speech.[12]

At the University of Colorado, political pressure from the legislature and governor's office quickly mounted on the administration and the governing board to investigate Churchill for his controversial remarks.[13] In late March, then-Interim Chancellor Philip DiStefano and two academic deans declared in a preliminary report that the inflammatory nature of Churchill's writings and speech was protected by constitutional rights and academic freedom, and could not be investigated as misconduct, but that other allegations of research misconduct could and should be the focus of a full investigation by the faculty's Standing Committee on Research Misconduct.[14] The investigations of two faculty panels eventually led to Churchill's firing in the summer of 2007.

I had written occasional blog entries on academic freedom after University of South Florida computer science faculty member Sami Al-Arian became a lightning rod for political attacks in late September 2001, with an appearance on the Bill O'Reilly show on Fox News. But the blog writing was still sparse for several years after the start of the Al-Arian controversy at USF. My first blog entry discussing academic freedom in 2004–2005 came in early November, in response to a local newspaper column written by an adjunct faculty member.[15] Below is a short table that documents the growth in my blog writing about academic freedom and in general during that academic year.

Table 6.1. Blog entries on academic freedom and in general, Sherman Dorn eponymous blog, 2004–2005 academic year.

Month	Academic-freedom entries	Other entries	All entries
September	0	0	0
October	0	2	2
November	2	3	5
December	0	5	5
January	2	11	13
February	4	10	14
March	13	4	17
April	15	7	22
May	12	8	20
9/2004–5/2005	48	50	98

Source: http://www.shermandorn.com

As Rep. Baxley filed the Academic Bill of Rights in January 2005, and during the controversy over Ward Churchill in February and later months, I found myself writing short and moderate-length comments on news of the day. This is a different type of writing from the coin of the realm for historians: the detailed historical argument supported by an archival and other documentary record. To comment on a news story, I had to jettison the level of careful research my doctoral program had trained me for. Instead, the typical pattern for writing became a quick reference to one or a few recent events and then a discussion of deeper principles or issues involved. In most of my entries, I used a current event as a springboard to discuss relevant research or historical perspectives. For example, with the breaking news of allegations of plagiarism against Churchill, I wrote three paragraphs with the title "And now, the plagiarism accusation":

> Thanks to Ralph Lukei for pointing out new allegations that Ward Churchill plagiarized work by a Canadian writer; according to the report, when she refused to have her work in one of his edited works appear in a second publication, he wrote something under his name that was remarkably similar. This may be part of a larger pattern of sloppy scholarship, if journalists' reports are accurate.

> And therein lies the crux of the matter: what has Ward Churchill's behavior been like as an academic? In my experience, good journalists "get it right" about 70–80 percent of the time. After all, if Phil Graham was correct that news was the first draft of history, that means there's plenty of rewriting to be done. So we take the allegations as printed in the media with a grain of salt. With claims of fraud, it's sometimes tough to find the truth, and as I've written before, academics can lie about each other and requires [sic] some care in investigation. Plagiarism is much easier to discern: compare the material. Sloppy footnoting is one thing, but stealing words is another.

> If Churchill has come close to or crossed the line over to plagiarism, I suspect he'll quickly agree to a buy-out now that these allegations exist.[16]

My larger point in the entry was that I would suspend judgment on the allegation because academics should not rely on the complete accuracy of news reporting. There are several differences between this informal writing and my more formal academic prose: the inclusion of contractions, colloquial expressions, and elliptical references to relevant outside material (the original entry has hyperlinks to relevant sources). My goal for the entry was to explain why many academics were unlikely to comment on the allegations in a manner more accessible than references to academic due process, trading a touch of breeziness for accessibility (or what I hoped would be accessible writing).

I have retained that pattern over the past decade, regularly writing entries in my blog that comment on news of the day. Since the spring of 2005, the bulk of my entries have focused on K–12 education policy. As one of the few academics regularly blogging on education policy in my state, I serve a niche audience—a public role that allows me the freedom to provide perspectives on current issues that are rarely explored in public. In this role, I complement journalism and nonacademic advocacy, as do other bloggers whose areas of expertise overlap with mine. There are other historians of education who blog, such as Diane Ravitch and Larry Cuban. Ravitch is generally known as a former center-right appointee of the first Bush administration who has turned against high-stakes testing; her academic background is used as an identifier more than a description of what her blog is about (it also focuses on education policy but with relatively little about history). Cuban is well known as a historian of education, and he writes longer essays than I do, and less frequently. Some sociologists of education also write blogs that focus on education policy, such as Sara Goldrick-Rab of the University of Wisconsin-Madison and Aaron Pallas of Teachers College, Columbia University. Jennifer Jennings wrote an anonymous blog as "Eduwonkette" while she was a doctoral student in the Columbia University sociology department; *Eduwonkette* was one of the most exciting and discussed education policy blogs for the short time it was active.

Slowly, my blog attracted attention. Horowitz's *FrontPageMag* incorrectly identified me as a Ward Churchill "champion" in late February 2005, and I began corresponding with others active across the country in academic-freedom disputes.[17] To the extent one can use website visitor data—very cautiously—my blog picked up a steady if small readership in Spring 2005. When I first moved my blog from *LiveJournal* to my eponymous domain name in late 2003, I had few visitors: 120 visits to the blog in all of December 2003, with 2 visits to any individual entry. In December 2004, I had 659 visitors to the blog, with 31 that month to the most "popular" individual entry, a criticism of a George Will column attacking faculty.[18] Three months later, I had 1,535 visitors, an average of 181 visits per day, and several entries with 50 or more visits. In the entire world, this is a small audience, but that audience has remained consistent. In March 2006, my blog had 3,855 separate visitors, 5,078 a year later, and 7,509 in March 2008. Today, my blog consistently receives a little over 1,000 visitors per day, with between 4,000 and 8,000 unique visitors each month (excluding automated hits such as from search robots). One of the small parts of my niche readership includes education reporters, and while my research (recent education policy history) is occasionally newsworthy, I know that the occasional call I receive from a reporter is due primarily to my blogging rather than my academic writing.

In the realm of academic blogs, my readership and any potential influence I may have is small potatoes compared to individual blogs such as Michael Bérubé's now-archived site[19] or group blogs such as the *Volokh Conspiracy*[20] and *Crooked Timber*.[21] It is also vastly larger than the circulation of hundreds of subscription-based refereed journals. The extent of audience and commenting (relatively light) shapes the conversation around what I write, but not the possibilities of academic blogging. When academics learn how to respond to news of the day, that engagement with current issues provides an opportunity for a rolling informal seminar, open to anyone who wants to read it or take part in an open conversation in comments. The openness of a blogging platform makes a blog a potential "naked seminar," stripped of the walls and clothing of a classroom setting. Because of the ease of publication, academic blogs are working effectively "without a net" of editing and peer review. Because it is public, writing for a blog is not the private act of classroom teaching. But blogging is nonetheless an act of public education in the broadest sense, comprising presentation of ideas with the possibility for extended conversation. Much of the discussion of blogs' contribution to intellectual life is about the liveliness of exchanges and the discarding of status symbols in return for that exchange.

As Paul Krugman has noted, intellectual blogging builds on a long tradition of informal interchange in many disciplines.[22] The result is that the "blogosphere" (and more generally quick publishing online) opens up that conversation from what was previously closely held to a public debate. There is no guarantee of the quality of the debate, but inconsistency is a trait of debates in refereed journals as well as debates in academic blogs. Some have slotted academic blogging into the category of "gray literature"; Michael Bérubé's observation that the writing in blogs can range from "raw" to "cooked" is perhaps the best summary description of that style range.[23] Within a single corpus (a website that readers would identify as a blog), the level of formality and consideration can range further, for nothing prohibits an author from deciding one day to write a two-sentence response to an event and type a 5,000-word essay the next. When academic blogs encourage comments, the goal is an engaged intellectual conversation.

How else would one describe a seminar?

NOTES

1. *The Last Intellectuals: American Culture in the Age of Academe* (New York: Basic Books, 2000), p. x.
2. Michael Wesch, *A Vision of Students Today* [video], October 12, 2007, available at http://www. youtube.com/watch?v=dGCJ46vyR9o; Sara Rimer, "At 71, Physics Professor Is a Web Star," *The New York Times*, December 19, 2007, available at http://www.nytimes.com/2007/12/19/ education/19physics.html
3. I also created (and continue to have) a separate LiveJournal account for personal entries. LiveJournal began operations in 1999; LiveJournal, Inc., "Frequently Asked Question #4" [webpage], November 23, 2010, retrieved from http://www.livejournal.com/support/faqbrowse. bml?faqid=4&view=full
4. The Horowitz campaign is best seen in the context of other attacks on academia in 2001 and later, especially an inflammatory "report" in late 2001 on supposedly disloyal professors issued by the American Council of Trustees and Alumni. For a broader discussion see Michael Bérubé, *What's Liberal About the Liberal Arts? Classroom Politics and "Bias" in Higher Education* (New York: W.W. Norton, 2006); and Greg McColm and Sherman Dorn, "A University's Dilemma in the Age of National Security," *Thought and Action*, Fall 2005, 163–177, retrieved from http://www. nea.org/assets/img/PubThoughtAndAction/TAA_05_16.pdf
5. H. Con. Res. 318, legislative tracking, retrieved from http://thomas.loc.gov/cgi-bin/bdquery/ z?d108:H.CON.RES.318: The bill was co-sponsored by 36 members of the House.
6. A Republican Florida Senate staff member commented in that chamber's bill analysis: "The bill elevates student expectations in academic instruction to the level of an academic freedom protected by the courts. Arguably, this academic freedom of students has not been recognized as a constitutional right. However, the bill appears to create a cause of action for students to litigate against the public postsecondary education institution in which they are enrolled. This cause of action could produce some unintended consequences. For example, in a course on study of the bible, a student could file suit demanding that the professor discuss evolution"; Senate Staff Analysis and Economic Impact Statement [on Senate Bill 2126], April 9, 2005, p. 4, retrieved from http://archive.flsenate.gov/data/session/2005/Senate/bills/analysis/pdf/2005s2126.ed.pdf. The flippant example provided in the analysis was a clue that Senate staff were dismissive of the bill once its flaws were brought to their attention late in the session. For an early analysis of the Academic Bill of Rights, see the American Association of University Professors Committee A on Academic Freedom and Tenure, "Statement on Academic Bill of Rights," December 2003, retrieved from http://www.aaup.org/AAUP/comm/rep/A/abor.htm
7. Center for Media and Democracy, "Academic Bill of Rights for Public Higher Education Act" documentation, n.d., retrieved from http://www.alecexposed.org/w/images/0/0d/2B1-Academic_Bill_of_Rights_for_Public_Higher_Education_ACT_Exposed.pdf
8. Forty-one of the 56 members of the Georgia Senate voted for the bill; see archived legislation page by the Georgia conference of the American Association of University Professors, retrieved from http://aaup.gcsu.edu/aaupgeorgiasenateresolution661.htm; "Assault on Faculty Heats Up!" *E-Newsletter of the California Conference of the American Association of University Professors*, January 2005, retrieved from http://www.aaup-ca.org/04-05Newsletter.html
9. I later discovered that Baxley's house shared a back fence with my mother-in-law's home in Ocala, Florida.
10. David Andreatta, "'WTC Nazi' Prof Invited," *New York Post*, January 27, 2005, retrieved from Lexis-Nexis Academic.

11. Churchill, "'Some People Push Back': On the Justice of Roosting Chickens," in *S11: Truth and Consequences* (Montreal: Kersplebedeb), retrieved from http://www.kersplebedeb.com/mystuff/s11/churchill.html

12. Patrick D. Healy, "College Cancels Speech over 9/11 Remarks," *The New York Times*, February 2, 2005.

13. Michelle York, "Professor Is Assailed by Legislature and Vandals," *The New York Times*, February 3, 2005; Valerie Richardson, "Colorado's Owens Urges Firing of 'Evil' Professor," *The Washington Times*, February 3, 2005; Richardson, "Regents To Examine Professor," *The Washington Times*, February 4, 2005.

14. Kirk Johnson, "University Changes Its Focus in Investigation of Professor," *The New York Times*, March 26, 2005; Philip DiStefano, Todd Gleeson, and David H. Getches, *Report on Conclusion of Preliminary Review in the Matter of Professor Ward Churchill*, March 24, 2005, retrieved from http://www.colorado.edu/news/reports/churchill/report.html

15. Lynn Stratton, "University of Silence in Florida," *St. Petersburg Times*, November 1, 2004, retrieved from http://www.sptimes.com/2004/11/01/Floridian/USF__University_of_Si.shtml; my response was "Academic-Freedom Juggling," November 2, 2004, retrieved from http://shermandorn.com/wordpress/?p=245.

16. "And Now, the Plagiarism Accusation," March 12, 2005, retrieved from http://shermandorn.com/wordpress/?p=288. My prediction was wildly inaccurate: Churchill fought the research misconduct charges both before and after his firing.

17. Jacob Laksin, "Churchill's Champions," *FrontPageMag*, February 28, 2005, retrieved from http://archive.frontpagemag.com/readArticle.aspx?ARTID=9423

18. "See George Dissemble," November 29, 2004, retrieved from http://shermandorn.com/wordpress/?p=247

19. http://www.michaelberube.com

20. http://volokh.com

21. http://crookedtimber.org

22. Paul Krugman, "Our Blogs, Ourselves" [blog entry], *The Conscience of a Liberal*, October 18, 2011, retrieved from http://krugman.blogs.nytimes.com/2011/10/18/our-blogs-ourselves/

23. Michael Bérubé, "The Sense of an Ending" [blog entry], August 10, 2005, retrieved from http://www.michaelberube.com/index.php/weblog/the_sense_of_an_ending/

CHAPTER SEVEN

The Public Intellectual

The Changing Context; Implications for Attributes and Practices

WILLIAM J. MATHIS

INTRODUCTION

The sledgehammer rose slowly before crashing into the windshield of the faded red SUV. Political opponents had bought Cheryl Rivers's old car, parked it in front of the statehouse, and proceeded to pound it to pieces. It made for dramatic television. Where other politicians had gone to ground, State Senator Rivers publicly defended Act 60, Vermont's new education funding law, and faced the critics of the legislation and the ensuing media firestorm head-on. As her frequent co-presenter, I learned that public forums jam-packed with people with their blood up do not have much in common with the cordial intellectual dialogue that (sometimes) occurs in academic circles.

I was luckier. I escaped with only one punctured tire in a dark, cold, snow-covered parking lot. I had had other brushes with public anger: my mailbox disappeared one night, and in another incident, the Ku Klux Klan burned down our camp gate and left us a little note. Anyone taking stands on public issues is subject to criticism, public scorn, and worse. It's exciting and scary, yet morally compelling. A good deal has been written about public intellectuals. The common thread is they bring a body of academic or scientific knowledge to bear on public policy issues and present this information to lay audiences in straightforward colloquial terms.

Or, to put it another way, it could be described as the translation of jargon-riddled, dense, intellectual gibberish into comprehensible language understandable and actionable by the public and policymakers. For instance, there's no real reason to expect policymakers (or most people) to understand the purpose of and techniques used in a "regression discontinuity analysis," but they can readily understand issues of equality and fairness. It's the public intellectual's job to translate arcane research language into language that is understandable, informative, and actionable.

I posit another criterion of a personal sort: the issue must be driven and take its force from fundamental values; it must have an explicit connection to improving society, increasing equality, and ensuring a democratic society. There are two objections that could be leveled against this principle. The first is: Who says democracy and equality are good things? For instance, a strict economic perspective could argue that the market model is completely value free. This would mean, of course, that civilization is driven strictly by monetary self-interest—a point that has a great implicit value assumption itself. The second objection is that my inclusion of values means that I have a negative bias—from the critic's perspective. This is easily addressed by pointing out that they also represent a bias. However, my views are founded in an egalitarian and democratic world. While they may make the same claim, this disagreement is exactly the debate that needs to take place in public policy discourse. To wit, what is the good, how do we know it, and will the issue at hand improve the common good?

The debate must also make a real difference in social policy and must be addressed on these grounds. On the face of things, academics would seem among the most qualified to be public intellectuals. In reality, this is not always the case. Some simply don't want to take the personal risk and find warm safety deep in the footnotes. Others focus on worthy topics but not on public policy. For example, comparing different phonics programs is a technical rather than a public policy issue. Higher education is also a bit of an institutional culprit. The quest for tenure or landing that big grant debilitates otherwise capable thinkers, making them overly cautious or too accommodating to the funding source. The purpose of being a public intellectual is not to add lines of peer-reviewed articles to your curriculum vita. It isn't about promotion to a higher academic rank or position. It must engage controversial public issues, and this involves taking risks.

In this brief essay, I focus more narrowly on the public intellectual's role in educational policy. I further concentrate on "within-the-field" work as contrasted to commentary coming from outside the field of education (media personalities, think tanks, and policymakers).

THE CHANGING POLICY CONTEXT: SOME HISTORY

Perhaps the epitome of the public intellectual was the remarkably influential "Metaphysical Club" of the late nineteenth century that brought together thinkers such as Oliver Wendell Holmes, William James, Charles Sanders Peirce, and John Dewey to debate the great issues of the day (Menand, 2001).

Traditionally, educational policy was determined by local school districts. In the last half of the twentieth century, state control over schools expanded as school finance litigation and statewide testing programs emerged. The federal government took on a useful and benign financial assistance role with the Elementary and Secondary Education Act in 1965 and the Education of All Handicapped Children Act in 1975 (94–142), which provided limited special-purpose funds to states. These efforts were transformed by the top-down, test-based accountability systems of Goals 2000 and were dramatically expanded by the No Child Left Behind Act of 2001. The Obama administration's use of state waivers to drive policy initiatives such as test-based teacher evaluation and common core state standards (which, despite denials, is a national curriculum) has resulted in a pronounced shift in the locus of policymaking—and thus changed the venue for the public intellectual (Henig, 2013; Cremin, 1988; Rothman, 2011; Mathis, 2012).

The political dialog on education has shifted from local school boards and communities to state and federal governments. This, in turn, has changed the media communications dynamic. It is less personal, harder to access, and mediated by a cornucopia of new electronic media from blogs to social media. Issues are more distorted and shaped more by lobbyists, think tanks, and those with economic interests in certain outcomes.[1]

The Decline of the Ivory Tower in Educational Policymaking

It was certainly true for the nineteenth century and for most of the twentieth century that the Ivory Tower was the lair of the public intellectual. This is changing in a number of ways.[2] Policy discourse has largely been excised from colleges of education. In the middle of the twentieth century, education foundations courses (mainly history and philosophy) were mainstay requirements for aspiring educators. Issues such as the purpose of education, what should be taught, and how it should be taught were debated. While a strong social justice perspective exists in some colleges, by the first part of the twenty-first century, foundations courses were virtually eliminated from educator preparation. Also gone are numerous foundations departments and professors who addressed these vital policy issues.[3] Instead, driven by groups such as NCATE, the preparation of teachers was, in many places, reduced to cobbling together the instructional skills necessary for teaching the Common Core State Standards and passing one of the national tests.

Some reformers, such as Art Wise, argue that most teacher education programs should be eliminated. Teach for America fundamentally dispenses with teacher training. While some institutions do maintain these perspectives to some degree, the door is basically closed on fundamental intellectual issues for a new generation of teachers.

The Rise of Partisan Think Tanks

As the prominence of college-based intellectuals descended, vested-interest, ideological, and partisan think tanks ascended. Supported by wealthy donors, these groups are generally oriented toward free-market philosophies. Those pushing neoliberal or conservative perspectives vastly outnumber those with a progressive or liberal orientation (Posner, 2003).

The main products of these denizens of K Street in Washington, D.C., are researchy-looking reports often presented in academese and garnished lavishly with footnotes, graphics, and statistical esoterica, and that are very aggressively marketed to policymakers through publications, lobbyists, Public Relations (PR) firms, forums, webinars, and seminars. Perhaps the most prolific is the conservative American Legislative Exchange Council. The partisan think tank groups have shown a remarkable ability to influence state and national politicians and, it can be argued, have far greater influence than traditional education organizations such as teacher unions, which are often dismissed as "defenders of the status quo."

While many members of these groups would lay claim to being "Public Intellectuals," the partisan nature of their organizations and publications belies any claim of scientific objectivity. That is, the intellectuals are hired hands to promote a given policy perspective. This bias gave rise to the Think Tank Review Project of the National Education Policy Center, which reviews the quality of these reports. (Full disclosure: this author works for NEPC.)[4]

The rise of the oligarchy: The Billionaire Boys' Club. Funding and supporting the think tanks are what Diane Ravitch calls the Billionaire Boys' Club.[5] For example, the Bill and Melinda Gates Foundation invested over $50 million in researching the use of test scores in teacher evaluations. The results from these studies are weak, but the concept remains a central tenet of Secretary of Education Arne Duncan's reform agenda.[6] The Eli Broad Foundation emphasizes recruiting education "leaders" from the military and business. They train these folks in a narrow, test-based, and essentialist philosophy of education. Similarly, the Friedman Foundation has focused on advancing school choice and goes from state to state administering clone surveys, which, unsurprisingly, find great support for school choice.

The decline of common media. With personal electronic devices and hundreds of television channels, communications media have dramatically changed, and continue to change. Paradoxically, with instantaneous connection to the world, the commonality of knowledge and messages becomes remarkably singular and isolated. With the rise of single-purpose television channels, society easily becomes insular and divided. The lack of common communication raises the question of whether democracy can be sustained with a Balkanized society.

"A free press exists as long as you own one" still applies, even though newspapers have declined in number and circulation. In education, "American education's newspaper of record" (*Education Week*) faces financial challenges and now hosts a full page of funders—which, not surprisingly, includes many of the same names as the billionaire boys' club. Advertising is concentrated on professional development courses, workshops, webinars, and alternate or neoliberal-oriented higher education offerings. Not surprisingly, the news coverage tends to favor the agenda of the funders and the advertisers.

Privatizing government. Democracy requires participation. Yet in recent educational policy debates, the democratic process has been sidestepped. The people have been removed from the governance process.

The most striking example of this is the formation of the Common Core State Standards. The National Governors Association and the Council of Chief State School Officers wished to adopt national standards and tests in the 1990s but immediately ran into intense political opposition. They then built and sheltered a private corporation, ACHIEVE, Inc., with private funding and government grants to achieve policy goals they could not achieve through representative public governance. As those pesky educators had very different ideas about curriculum, the mainstream education organizations were simply excluded. The standards were formulated in a closed process with only nominal and tightly controlled external review procedures. Participants had to sign a non-disclosure agreement.

The standards were then trotted through state boards of education (and some states adopted them before they were complete), generally without hearings or close examination. The standards (beyond the claim of being internationally competitive) were never benchmarked (validated) in any demonstrable way. The core claim that "high standards" would improve states or nations suffers from a lack of empirical support.

Thus, the goals, standards, and assessments—the very purposes of education in a democracy—were removed from the public deliberation process. Public debate by public intellectuals (or by elected representatives) was sidestepped.[7]

The Co-Optation of the Education Organizations

"Sitting at the table doesn't make you a diner, unless you eat some of what's on that plate."
—MALCOLM X, 1965

In the strange miasma afflicting those circumscribed by the beltway, the level of public discourse has markedly declined. The organizations no longer lead educational policy thought, and they have even failed to be an effective loyal opposition.

They have become accommodationists parroting phrases like "unless we adopt and support XYZ" (such as test-based teacher evaluation), we will "lose our seat at the table." Regrettably, political trimming and posturing is ascendant over thoughtful discourse and the careful review of research findings. For the public intellectual, when the evidence says the plan doesn't work or is downright harmful, maybe it's better to stand than to sit at that table.

ATTRIBUTES OF THE PUBLIC INTELLECTUAL

Such a formidable change in how public education policy is made and who can shape it poses new challenges for the public intellectual. This essay presumes that being a public intellectual is a good thing and that we need to encourage others in this endeavor. These changed conditions have implications for the job requirements.

The necessary job skills and personal attributes of the public intellectual are:

- Above all else, a deep commitment to public education, equity, and equality.
- A fire in the belly and a willingness to act.
- Deep training in research methods and statistics is desirable but not essential. If not deeply trained, the willingness to consult with others who have deeper understandings of the methodology or content.
- The ability and willingness to read technical and research documents with a discerning eye for solid work vs. eyewash.
- The ability to translate research gibberish into language easily comprehended by lay readers and policymakers.
- An ability to write in both technical and non-technical ways that vividly, accurately, and succinctly capture the issues at hand.
- The patience to check sources and go through countless revisions until you are certain you have it correct. From the writer's perspective, this means saying to yourself "That's good" rather than "That's good enough."
- The ability to throw away a paper after days of work when you realize it's crummy or it just didn't pan out.
- Being willing to risk being criticized or ridiculed. It doesn't happen very often, but it is certainly memorable when it does.
- Balanced thought and presentation. Undisciplined fulminations get you labeled and discredited as a wing-nut. Remember, your ultimate objective is to persuade.

POTENTIAL PRACTICES AND STRATEGIES

Establishing yourself as a credible voice takes some time but is easy enough to do if you think of it as a series of small, discrete steps. I base the following suggestions on my experience in multiple roles over the past 40 years, including academic, superintendent, researcher, and policymaker. If you are an academic, writing peer-reviewed and professional papers is one of the requirements of your job. Unfortunately, peer-reviewed journal articles seldom make a difference in policy, and they certainly are not widely read by the public. Instead, look at your professional papers as material to be mined for the important work of communicating with lay audiences and policymakers.

The Op-Ed and the Blog

Among the quickest and most effective ways of disseminating information is the op-ed or blog. These media require short, disciplined pieces typically running 600–750 (but no more than 900) words.[8]

If well written, op-ed pieces and blog postings have a much better chance of engaging your audience than do longer pieces. Poor or dull writing will either not be printed or, if printed, won't be read. The medium imposes a discipline on the writer for tight organization, strong leads, logical development, and a good close. Proofread, edit, and revise your work. Sleep overnight on the article. Articles that looked good yesterday often do not look so fine in the morning. If there is anything that makes the difference between good and bad writing, it is in the art of revision. Expect to take four or five sessions over several days to be satisfied with even a short column.

Use friends and relatives as sounding boards and reviewers of your work, but tell them what you are looking for or are worried about (organization, flow, clarity, etc.). Or, if you are basically finished and you just want them to favorably commend your opus for a Pulitzer Prize, tell them that. This can prevent divorces.

Currency is a requirement for op-eds, and the faster you can work off of a news story, the better. Some things such as test-based accountability have longer windows. But if you are featuring a study released a year ago or a poll from 6 months ago, there will be less interest in the article.

The public intellectual is often a counterpuncher reacting to notions that are politically popular. Getting in the same news window as the original stimulus means quick action.

Time the release so that print media will have the same advantage as the much faster electronic media. Talk to editors about when they need articles for the Sunday paper.

If you are not getting paid for the column or do not otherwise have an agreement with the publisher, you hold the copyright and can use the article in more than one place. Be careful, however, to honor any agreement you may have made or implied for exclusive use. Professional writing (as opposed to lay or popular media writing) has more restrictive protocols. Blogs go viral and are often copied without the author's permission. Expect this to happen.

Sometimes, but not always, you can use the same column for state as well as national media. But don't try to force it. What is current at the state level may not be current at the national level, and vice versa.

Other Venues to Consider

Successful column writing leads to other opportunities such as legislative testimony, speaking opportunities, and television follow-ups. Here are some other venues.

Radio and television. Public radio is an effective medium and has high listenership among policymakers. Even though radio and television media will not use a column, send it to them anyway. Once an issue is in the public eye, producers are looking for experts to interview. Often it is the local radio or cable access station that will be your entry point. Don't expect the National Press Club to call until you have a major book or you are involved in a high-profile activity.

Public programs and debates. Civic groups often organize programs on contemporary issues or need luncheon speakers. Keep in touch with these people. Sometimes they will arrange pro and con programs, and you find yourself squaring off against some of your least favorite people—who happen to embrace the polar opposite view. Be civil and courteous. Try not to make gaffes that will get you quoted in the opposition's media. By and large, it's a matter of who is the most well-informed and persuasive speaker. Preparation is important. In your remarks, be prepared for counterarguments and criticism, and always remember that it is about values and equality.

Presentations. Shop your presentations to professional associations and influential policy groups. In your remarks and materials, you have an obligation to be clear and absolutely accurate. If you are found to exaggerate or are factually wrong, expect to hear about it. It will harm your credibility. If you use or distribute information that some might consider to be generated by a paranoid wing-nut, you and your information will be discredited. Paradoxically, an amazing phenomenon is the intellectual casualness of many of the prominent, top-dollar national seminar presenters. Many of these people have no depth of knowledge in their field but are quite confident in their conclusions and in the breezy, polished way they express their views. I recommend you stay away from such Elmer Gantry approaches. Being wrong but slick may work, but it is ultimately dishonest.

Testimony. Check your state board and legislative committee schedules (something that often requires some web digging and personal phone calls or emails) and sign yourself up. Establish personal contacts with the chairs of these groups. Let them know you would like to speak on a given issue. Make sure you have the policymakers on your email lists.

Non-refereed writing. Often trade publications are looking for good articles. Check their websites and see if they are soliciting in your areas of expertise. Know who you are submitting to and the focus of that publication. Checking out the style of the publication is the most important single thing you can do to increase the probability of an acceptance.

Refereed articles. Refereed publications are important for your professional career; they help you to gain credibility and establish network contacts. Again, check the nature of the publication to make sure your topic and approach are compatible with the periodical's editorial policies. Bear in mind that research publications are not generally read by policymakers. Again, that doesn't mean you should not write them. Simply have a lay version of your findings for other media.

The executive summary and press releases. By the time an author gets to the summary or the press release, she is sick of looking at the article and simply wants it off her desk. This is not the place to rush for closure. Take extreme care in drafting, reviewing, and revising these final pieces. They are likely the only things that will get read. If they don't like your summary, they won't read the article. Your summary must capture the key components of the article or report.

Using and documenting the right sources. In my blog entries, I use hyperlinks that connect the reader to my sources. This adds credibility. As a general rule, avoid using sources that carry a bias. The more prestigious and sound the source, the more credible you become.

Inviting policymakers to events. In my classes, I invited governors, ex-governors, legislative chairs, and other influential political leaders to speak. Invite these people to your gatherings. This is flattering to the dignitary and will give you more personalized time and influence with them than you would otherwise receive.

Social media. Social media have proven themselves in terms of getting information out quickly. The greatest danger is that there is limited quality control (all kinds of things are put on the web). Further, there is a tendency to form communities limited to like-minded people. This leads to talking past each other. However, the jury is still out on whether and how social media will be an effective means of communication for the public intellectual.

CONCLUSIONS

It is in times of fuzzy information characterized by strong ideological, political, and economic divides that the work of the public intellectual is most essential. The stewardship of ideas, rooted in universal and democratic ideals, is not a political position. It is an empirically demonstrable necessity for the survival of a fractious and seemingly self-destructive world. To be effective, the public intellectual must focus with a singular eye upon the policymaking apparatus. This machinery now lies outside the traditional walls of schools, school districts, and the university.

With the ascendance of think tanks, ideologues, and concentrated wealth, it is a radically different policymaking process that must be addressed by taking the issues to the broader public and to the policymakers.

This calls for new skills and personal attributes, including vision, commitment, courage, and perseverance. The means of influence are still as personal as they always were, but the nature of contemporary society and communications means using electronic media as well.

In my engagement in the school finance wars, I wrote an article that asked, "When's the cavalry coming?" (Mathis, 2000). When you are being shot at out in the desert, you start looking over your shoulder and wondering where your *compadres* went. Putting yourself out there, being viciously attacked, and risking your job is a lonely business and not always the easiest thing to do. My own answer is that I believe it is the only worthwhile way to live a life and give it meaning.

Although you are existentially alone, your friends and colleagues are nevertheless the greatest source of support for you as a public intellectual. It is no accident that my closest professional colleagues are also public intellectuals and risk-takers. Also, there are networks. The attorneys and advocates who work for fair and equitable funding find each other, as do people with their own special interests. The bloggers know each other. In state and national organizations, friendships are found that go beyond official roles.

In the spirit of John Dewey, the goal of the public intellectual should be to support a democratic society characterized by equality and high-quality opportunities for every child. I think this is not only a worthy cause but also a moral imperative. That's why we need public intellectuals who are willing to enter the fray and ensure that debates are grounded in accurate data and credible research, and to ensure that policymaking supports the common good.

NOTES

1. For a sampling of the author's blog posts, think tank reviews, and policy briefs, go to http://nepc.colorado.edu/ and search on "Mathis."
2. See Henig (2013) for a lengthier examination. Also, review the websites of, for example, the Friedman Foundation, the Fordham Institute, and the American Enterprise Institute.
3. For a more expansive treatment, see Posner (2003).
4. See, for example, Gone But Not Forgotten: The Decline of History as an Educational Foundation, http://eric.ed.gov/?id=EJ910742
5. For examples of partisan think tanks' reports and reviews of their work, go to http://nepc.colorado.edu/think-tank-reviews
6. For example, see Strauss (2011).
7. Reviews of the three MET studies sponsored by Gates can be found at NEPC. Colorado.edu
8. This intentional process of not engaging the public or educators is described in the quasi-official history of the effort, Rothman (2011).

REFERENCES

Cremin, L.A. (1988). *American education: The metropolitan experience: 1876–1980*. New York: Harper & Row.

Henig, J.R. (2013). *The end of exceptionalism in education: The changing politics of school reform*. Cambridge, MA: Harvard Education Press.

Mathis, W.J. (2000, April). *Interest group influences in advancing and inhibiting educational finance reform*. Paper presented at the annual meeting of the American Educational Research Association, New Orleans, LA.

Mathis, W.J. (2012, February 20). The war on inequality, global inferiority & low standards: Common Core State Standards. *Education Review, 15*(1). [Review of the book Rothman, R. (2011). *Something in common: The Common Core State Standards*. Cambridge, MA: Harvard Education Press.]

Menand, L. (2001). *The Metaphysical Club: A story of ideas in America*. New York: Farrar, Straus, and Giroux.

Posner, R.A. (2003). *Public intellectuals: A study of decline*. Cambridge, MA: Harvard University Press.

Rothman, R. (2011). *Something in common: The Common Core State Standards*. Cambridge, MA: Harvard Education Press.

Strauss, V. (2011, November 15). Ravitch: Billionaires (and millionaires) for education reform. *The Washington Post*. Retrieved from http://www.washingtonpost.com/blogs/answer-sheet/post/ravitch-billionaires-and-millionaires-for-education-reform/2011/11/15/gIQAlDAHPN_blog.html

Personal Dilemmas

CHAPTER EIGHT

Reflections of a "Stunt Intellectual"

Caught in the Crosshairs of "Public" Controversy

WILLIAM AYERS

The idea of a set of creatures called "public intellectuals" has long puzzled me, especially when that label has been affixed to me, as it has on occasion. The term always seems just a bit too lofty for me. If I'm any kind of intellectual at all, I'd think to myself, I'm a "stunt intellectual," the guy the real intellectuals call when they have to jump off a bridge or hang upside down from the wing of an airplane.

It's true that I write—books, articles, chapters, reviews, op-eds, blog posts— and that I speak whenever I'm asked to at conferences, on campuses, and in community gatherings all over the place. It's true that I'm a life-long teacher and activist. It's also true that I'm an advocate for a culture of democracy and for the creation of an expansive and generous public square where people can come together as equals, face one another without masks, and engage in dialogue: listening with the possibility of being changed and speaking with the possibility of being heard. And it's also undeniable that my particular history and my ongoing activism have occasionally thrust me unwittingly into manufactured controversies not of my choosing. For example, in October 2008, officials at the University of Nebraska-Lincoln canceled three talks I was scheduled to give in mid-November at the College of Education. The college was celebrating its centennial that year, and a faculty committee determined that I could contribute in some way to the dialogue that marks these kinds of occasions. I was invited to prepare a paper on narrative research in schools and communities as part of a student research conference, and then to engage graduate students informally in a "fireside chat" about qualitative inquiry and their own research agendas, challenges, and demands. Finally, I was to give a keynote address, which I had tentatively called "We Are Each Other's Keepers: Research and Teaching to Change the World."

The day before the cancellation, and at the height of the presidential campaign, an administrator called me to say that my pending visit was causing a "firestorm." She said that the governor, a U.S. senator, and the chairman of the Board of Regents had all issued statements condemning the decision to invite me to campus.

The president of the university said, "While I believe that the open exchange of ideas and the principles of academic freedom are fundamental to a university, I also believe the decision to have Ayers on a program to celebrate the college's centennial represents remarkably poor judgment." The Regents chairman added that while he welcomed controversial viewpoints, "The authority we grant to the faculty to decide what to teach and who to invite comes with a responsibility to use that authority and that freedom with sound judgment. In this case, I think, that was violated." That struck me as worthy of the disciplinarian of a middle school commenting on a decision about homecoming made by the student council.

The administrator told me further that the university was receiving vicious emails and threatening letters, as well as promises of physical disruption from anonymous sources were I to show up. She said that the university's "threat assessment group" (yipes!) had identified "serious safety concerns."

I sympathized and told her how terribly sorry I was that all of this was happening to them. I also said that I thought it was a bit of a tempest in a teapot, and that it would surely pass. Certainly, no matter what a group of extremists claimed they might do, I said, I thought that the Nebraska state police could get me to the podium, and I would handle myself from there.

She wasn't so sure. And who knows? I'm not from Nebraska.

Still, I said, I thought we should stand together and refuse to accede to these kinds of pressures. Is a public university the personal fiefdom or the political clubhouse of the governor? Are there things we dare not name if they happen to offend a donor? Do we institute a political litmus test or a background check on every guest? Do we collapse in fear if a small mob gathers with torches at the gates? I wouldn't force myself on the college, of course, but I felt that canceling would send a terrible message to students, bring shame to the university, and be another step down the slippery slope of giving up on the precious ideal of a free university in a free society.

It's hard to think what consistently rational argument could have been advanced in the halls of power for canceling my scheduled time in Lincoln. That I'm not a patriot? My loving the country includes speaking up, engaging in the public square, and opposing injustice as a personal and political responsibility. It requires resisting any mindless or thoughtless avoidance of the dreadful things that our government has done and continues to do. Future generations will decide who the true patriots were, for example, during the Vietnam years: those veterans who threw their medals at the White House, those who had the courage to refuse to fight an illegal and murderous war, those who suffer in silence at home today, or those who claim to know which part of America is "the real America?"

That I'm an unrepentant terrorist with no regrets? I am not and never was a terrorist. Terrorists use indiscriminate violence and target the innocent, intending to kill and engender fear among people. Nothing I did 40 years ago was terrorism; the fact is that no one was killed or even injured by any actions of the Weather Underground, an illegal organization I was indeed part of. We were militant, to be sure; we crossed lines of legality and perhaps even common sense. But we were not terrorists. By contrast, the invasion and occupation of Vietnam, at the cost of thousands of innocents killed every week for 10 years, was indeed an instance of unspeakable terror.

I make no claim that violence should be part of any progressive movement; indeed, I believe that nonviolent direct action is a powerful tool for social change. But I must note here that our government has been the greatest purveyor of violence on earth, as the Rev. Martin Luther King, Jr., said in 1967. We live in fact in a sewer of violence, often exported, always rationalized and hidden through mystification and the frenzied use of bread and circuses. If opposing all violence is the oath that must be spoken in order to come to Lincoln, I said at the time, consider who will be excluded: both of Nebraska's U.S. senators, the governor, the president and his entire cabinet, the liberal head of the New School, and the leaders of both major political parties, military recruiters, and anyone not a pacifist. And don't forget Nelson Mandela: he wasn't in prison all those years merely for acts of civil disobedience.

I am a political radical, a lifelong educator, public scholar, and skeptic. But I'm not the least bit radioactive. It is true that I was made an issue in the 2008 presidential campaign, and that unwanted celebrity is absolutely the only reason I was not allowed to speak at the University of Nebraska. But the fallout affected me only marginally. The university suffers: after all, isn't the primary job of intellectuals and scholars to challenge orthodoxy, dogma, and mindless complacency, to be skeptical of all authoritative claims, to interrogate and trouble the given and the taken-for-granted? The growth of knowledge, insight, and understanding depends on that kind of effort, and the inevitable clash of ideas that follows must be nourished and not crushed. In this case Nebraska shunned its responsibility, and a faculty committee set up to look into the matter denounced the administration.

Again in April 2010, an invitation to speak to a legitimate campus group at the University of Wyoming was cancelled by the administration. Of course an invitation should in no way be interpreted as an endorsement, and inviting someone to campus could also serve as an opportunity to debate, to sharpen disagreements.

Further, I was in no way the injured party when my talk was cancelled. I spoke freely—to myself, my kids, my colleagues and students—and I was fine. The injured party was the group of faculty and students who wanted to engage me— for whatever reasons (and I have only the vaguest sense of who my original host was, or how the talk might have gone). It was their freedom, not mine, that was trampled out of misplaced fear or petty expediency, or both.

And then one wonders: if my ideas are so toxic in public arenas, shouldn't the noisy posse that shouted down the most basic values in a democracy press the university president to scour the library and purge it of all of my books? Perhaps he should head them off by getting there first, burning the books himself. Who else should be purged, and on what basis? Maybe convicted felons should be banned (I'm thinking Martha Stewart, George Ryan, G. Gordon Liddy, and Scooter Libby, but not me since I've never been convicted of a felony) or bad role models (all eye-of-the-beholder stuff, for sure, but I'm thinking Eliot Spitzer and Tiger Woods). And try to think, then, of what standard exists in the mind of a university president that impels him to ban me, and only me. What if the French Club invites Sarkozy, or the China Club Hu Jinao or Ha Jin, or the Literature Club Junot Diaz or James Frey or Arundhati Roy, or the Prison Rights Club Mark Clements or Ronnie Kitchens or Nelson Mandela? Should there be a panel to scrutinize every potential speaker and certify them as…what, exactly?

Anyway, there is something much greater at stake here than some small speech I might have delivered to 75 students. As campuses contract and constrain, the main victims become truth, honesty, integrity, curiosity, imagination, and freedom itself.

When college campuses fall silent on public debates, other victims include the high school history teacher on the west side of Chicago or in Laramie or Cheyenne, the English literature teacher in Detroit, or the math teacher in an Oakland middle school. They and countless others immediately get the message: be careful what you say; stay close to the official story; stick to the authorized text; keep quiet with your head covered.

The students sued in federal court, I joined the suit, and a right-wing judge enjoined the university and lectured the president on what freedom of expression means. I spoke to an audience of thousands instead of the handful that might have showed up in the first place. Oh, freedom.

And finally, when I retired from the University of Illinois at Chicago in 2010, the board of trustees, for the first time in history, voted to deny emeritus status, a routine request from the dean, provost chancellor, and president. I had been promoted to Senior University Scholar and Distinguished Professor of Education over the years, decisions affirmed by the board. But once again the noisy opposition was heard, and once again, while I don't feel that I suffered a bit, the attack on academic freedom seems plain enough to me, and the message is as clear: Be Careful!

Returning to my puzzlement concerning public intellectuals, it comes, I think, from two directions. One, it's hard to imagine what a *private* intellectual would look like—a recluse or a hermit, perhaps Emily Dickinson, but how public she has become!—and two, since all human beings are created with the capacity to critically reflect on their lives and on the world, and since each is a philosopher and an expert on his or her own life, it seems odd—and a little elitist—to exclude anyone from the fortress of the intellectuals. We all experience life, think, and learn—we are each and all of us, then, intellectuals.

Of course, some of us are employed or assigned to act as professional intellectuals—teachers, librarians, journalists, researchers—and it's worth exploring, then, the ethical dimensions, dilemmas, and moral responsibilities we take on when we assume those specific roles. For perspective I turn to the transcendent literary critic Edward Said—author of the essential text *Orientalism*—and his BBC lectures, collected in a brilliant text called *Representations of the Intellectual*. The book is crisp, concise, small in size—the perfect companion to cram into your backpack between your toothbrush and your bottle of water, and as necessary to daily survival as either of these, for in it Said offers in effect a brief for the ethical and lively conduct of intellectual life.

The intellectual, Said argues, must strive to become "an individual endowed with a faculty for representing, embodying, articulating a message, a view, an attitude, philosophy or opinion to, as well as for, a public" (Said, 1994, p. 11). The role has an edge to it, for the intellectual must open spaces "to raise embarrassing questions, to confront orthodoxy and dogma (rather than to produce them), to be someone who cannot easily be co-opted by governments or corporations, and whose *raison d'être* is to represent all those people and issues that are routinely forgotten or swept under the rug." This means searching out and fighting for relative independence from all manner of social and institutional pressures, to authentically choose oneself against a hard wall of facts. "At bottom," Said argues, "the intellectual…is neither a pacifier nor a consensus-builder, but someone whose whole being is staked on a critical…sense of being unwilling to accept easy formulas, or ready-made clichés, or the smooth, ever-so-accommodating confirmations of what the powerful or conventional have to say, and what they do." This unwillingness to accede cannot be simply a passive shrug or a cynical sigh; it absolutely must involve, as well, publicly staking out a space of refusal. Think of this as a standard for teachers to try to enact it in classrooms—K–12, college, and graduate school. There is nothing easy or automatic in accepting the mantle and then working it out in practice in a serious, sustained, and principled way.

The challenging intellectual work of teaching pivots on our ability to see students as three-dimensional creatures—human beings much like ourselves—with hopes and dreams, aspirations, skills, and capacities; with minds and hearts and spirits; with embodied experiences, histories, and stories to tell of a past and a possible future; with families, neighborhoods, cultural surrounds, and language communities all interacting, dynamic, and entangled. This knotty, complicated challenge requires patience, curiosity, wonder, awe, and more than a small dose of humility. It demands sustained focus, intelligent judgment, inquiry and investigation. It requires an open heart and an inquiring mind, since every judgment is contingent, every view partial, and each conclusion tentative. The student is dynamic, alive, and in motion; nothing is settled, once and for all. No perspective can ever be big enough, no summary ever entirely authoritative. The student grows and changes—yesterday's urgent need is suddenly accomplished and quickly forgotten, today's claims are all encompassing and brand new. This, then, is an intellectual task of massive proportion.

The challenge involves, as well, an ethical stance and an implied moral contract. The good teacher offers unblinking attention and communicates a deep regard for students' lives, a respect for both their integrity and their vulnerability. An engaged teacher begins with a belief that each student is unique, each the one and only one who will ever trod the earth, each worthy of a certain reverence. Regard extends, importantly, to an insistence that students have access to the tools with which to negotiate and perhaps even to transform the world. Love for students just as they are—without any drive or advance toward a future—is false love, enervating and disabling. The teacher must try, in good faith, to do no harm, and then to convince students to reach out, to reinvent, and to seize an education fit for the fullest lives they might hope for.

With eyes wide open and riveted on learners, a further challenge is to stay wide awake to the world, to the concentric circles of context in which we and our students live and work. Teachers must know and care about some aspect of our shared life—our calling, after all, is to shepherd and enable the callings of others. Teachers, then, invite students to become somehow more capable, more thoughtful and powerful in their choices, more engaged in a culture and a civilization, able to participate, to embrace—and yes, to change all that is before them. How do we warrant that invitation? How do we understand this society and our culture?

Teachers choose. They choose how to see the students before them. They choose how to see the world; what to embrace and what to reject; whether to support or resist this or that directive. In schools where the insistent illusion that everything has already been settled is heavily promoted, teachers and students alike experience a constricted sense of choice, diminished imaginative space, a feeling of powerlessness regarding the larger purposes of education. Said exhorts intellectuals—for us, teachers and educators—to work on the basis of a principle he takes to be universal: "that all human beings are entitled to expect decent standards of behavior concerning freedom and justice from worldly powers or nations [including all institutions—schools, for example, or corporations], and that deliberate or inadvertent violations of these standards need to be testified to and fought against courageously" (Said, 1994, pp. 11–12). This exhortation does not provide any particular comfort, nor does it lay out a neat road forward, for if you choose the path of opposition, you do not inherit a set of ready-made slogans or a nifty, easy-fit party line. There are no certainties, no gods whatsoever who can be called upon to ease specific, personal responsibility, to settle things once and for all. Each of us is out there on our own, with our own minds and our own hearts, our own ability to empathize, to touch and to feel, to recognize humanity in its many unexpected postures, to construct our own standards of truth about human suffering that must be upheld despite everything. "Real intellectuals," Said writes, "are never more themselves than when, moved by metaphysical passion and disinterested principles of justice and truth, they denounce corruption, defend the weak, defy imperfect or oppressive authority" (p. 6). Said is uninterested in allying with the victors and the rulers whose very stability he sees as a certain kind of "state of emergency" for the less fortunate; he chooses instead to account for "the experience of subordination itself, as well as the memory of forgotten voices and persons."

In the world of teaching and learning, schooling and education, Said's concept of the intellectual's role resonates with particular force. We live in a time when the assault on disadvantaged communities is particularly harsh and at the same time gallingly obfuscated. Access to adequate resources and decent facilities, to relevant curriculum, to opportunities to reflect on and think critically about the world and one's place within it is unevenly distributed along predictable lines of class and color. Further, a movement to dismantle public schools under the rubric of "standards and accountability" is in place and gaining force. This is the moment in which we have to choose who to be as scholars and intellectuals, as teachers and researchers, and as citizens.

The current frontal attack on public education is an attack on democracy itself. Education is a perennial battleground, for this is where we ask ourselves who we are as people, what it means to be human here and now, and what world we hope to inhabit. It's where we assess our chances and access our choices, and it's where we take up dynamic questions of morality and ethics, identity and location, agency and action.

The unique characteristic of education in a democracy is a commitment to a particularly precious and fragile ideal, and that is a belief that the fullest development of all is the necessary condition for the full development of each; conversely, the fullest development of each is necessary for the full development of all. Education is an enterprise that rests on the twin pillars of enlightenment and liberation, knowledge and human freedom. We want to know more, to see more, to experience more in order to do more—to be more competent and powerful and capable in our projects and our pursuits, to be more astute and aware and wide awake, more fully engaged in the world that we inherit, the world we are simultaneously destined to change. To deny students the right to question the circumstances of their lives, and to wonder how they might be otherwise, is to deny democracy itself.

Democracy, after all, is geared toward participation and engagement, and it's based on a common faith: every human being is of infinite and incalculable value, each a unique intellectual, emotional, physical, spiritual, and creative force. Every human being is born free and equal in dignity and rights; each is endowed with reason and conscience and deserves, then, a sense of solidarity, brotherhood and sisterhood, recognition and respect.

We want our students to be able to think for themselves, to make judgments based on evidence and argument, to develop minds of their own. We want them to ask fundamental questions—Who in the world am I? How did I get here and where am I going? What in the world are my choices? How in the world shall I proceed?—and to pursue answers wherever they might take them. Democratic educators focus their efforts not on the production of things so much as on the production of fully developed human beings who are capable of controlling and transforming their own lives, citizens who can participate fully in civic life.

Democratic teaching encourages students to develop initiative and imagination, the capacity to name the world, to identify the obstacles to their full humanity, and the courage to act upon whatever the known demands. Education in a democracy should be characteristically eye-popping and mind-blowing—always about opening doors and opening minds as students forge their own pathways into a wider world.

Much of what we call schooling forecloses or shuts down or walls off meaningful choice making. Much of it is based on obedience and conformity, the hallmarks of every authoritarian regime. Much of it banishes the unpopular, squirms in the presence of the unorthodox, hides the unpleasant. There's no space for skepticism, irreverence, or even doubt. While many of us long for teaching as something transcendent and powerful, we find ourselves too often locked in situations that reduce teaching to a kind of glorified clerking, passing along a curriculum of received wisdom and predigested and often false bits of information. In the long run this is a recipe for disaster.

Educators, students, and citizens—public intellectuals—must press for an education worthy of a democracy, including an end to sorting people into winners and losers through expensive standardized tests that act as pseudo-scientific forms of surveillance; an end to starving schools of needed resources and then blaming teachers for dismal outcomes; and an end to the rapidly accumulating "educational debt," the resources due to communities historically segregated, under-funded, and under-served. All children and youth in a democracy, regardless of economic circumstance, deserve full access to richly resourced classrooms led by caring, qualified, and generously compensated teachers.

We might declare that in this corner of this place—in this open space we are constructing together—people will begin to experience themselves as powerful authors of their own narratives, actors in their own dramas, the essential architects and creators of their own lives, participants in a dynamic and interconnected community-in-the-making. Here they will discover a zillion ways to articulate their own desires and demands and questions. Here everyone will live *in search of* rather than *in accordance with* or *in accommodation to*. As we wrangle over what to pass on to the future generation and struggle over what to value and how, students must find vehicles and pathways to question the circumstances of their lives, and to wonder, individually and together, about how their lives might be otherwise. Free inquiry, free questioning, dialogue and struggle must take their rightful place—at the heart of things.

A delightful video emerged from student-led struggles in the spring of 2010 at the University of California organized to resist the grinding and relentless undoing of public higher education. A student attends to her daily routine, writing, reading, sitting in a lecture hall, while the camera focuses here and there, and a voice-over intones: "Pen: $1.69; Textbook: $38; Backpack: $69; Dinner (a tiny packet of dry noodles!): $.50...." And at the end of the list: "Education [pause]... Priceless." The tag-line is perfect: "There are some things that money can't buy; don't let education be one of them."

The crisis in public higher education, like the crisis in K–12 schooling, is not a joke at all: tuition and fees are skyrocketing across the country and are already out of reach for millions; staff cut-backs, lay-offs, and reductions in student services have become commonplace; massive student loans have replaced grants and scholarships; class size is increasing while course offerings are decreasing; hiring freezes and pay cuts and unpaid mandatory furloughs are on the rise as tenure-track positions are eliminated. These and other "short-term" strategies for dealing with financial crisis are consistent with the overall direction that has characterized public higher education for decades: "restructuring" as biz-speak for a single-minded focus on the bottom line. And all of this is part of a larger crisis of the state, and larger choices about who pays and who suffers.

A few snapshots: state support for the University of Illinois system stands at about 16% today, down from 48% two decades ago. In California, state colleges will turn away 40,000 qualified students this year, while the community colleges, in a cascading effect, will turn away 100,000. And this year a 32% fee hike is proposed at the University of California, Berkeley (a proposal that triggered the current student movement there), while the school pays its football coach $2.8 million a year and is just completing a $400 million renovation of the football stadium.

These and similar trends are national in scope and impact. The average college graduate is between $20,000 and $30,000 in debt for student loans (not including credit-card and other debt), compared to $9,000 in 1994; Pell Grants cover less than 32% of annual college costs; less than 20% of graduate students are unionized, and student labor at below-market wages keeps the whole enterprise afloat;

tenured and tenure-track faculty are disappearing, today holding barely 30% of all faculty lines; out-of-state students are increasing in most public schools because they pay significantly higher tuition, and that pattern is turning public colleges and universities into "engines of inequality," places with both less access and less equity, less social justice and fewer highly qualified students—private schools in fact, remaining public in name only. This grim picture can be brought into sharper and more painful focus: California spends more on prisons than on higher education— across the country, spending on "corrections" is six times higher than spending on higher education—and from 1985 to 2000, Illinois increased spending on higher education by 30% while spending on corrections shot up 100%. Here we gain a clearer insight into the budget crises that are being rationalized and balanced on our heads: a permanent war economy married to a prison society, with the abused and neglected offspring paying for the sins of the parents.

Said speaks for a particular stance, a distinct approach to intellectual life. All intellectuals, he argues, "represent something to their audiences, and in so doing represent themselves to themselves" (1994, p. xv). Whether you're a straight-up academic or a freelance writer, a down-and-out bohemian essayist or an itinerant speechmaker, an educational researcher or a teacher or a consultant to corporations or the state, you represent yourself based on an idea you have of yourself and your function: Do you think you're providing a balanced, disinterested view, or are you delivering objective advice for pay? Are you an expert offering high-level program evaluation, or are you teaching your students some indispensible truth? Perhaps you imagine you're advocating an eccentric if important idea. What do you want to represent? To whom? For what purpose? Toward what end, and in the interest of what social order?

"It is a spirit in opposition, rather than in accommodation," Said writes, "that grips me because the romance, the interest, the challenge of intellectual life is to be found in dissent against the status quo at a time when the struggle on behalf of underrepresented and disadvantaged groups seems so unfairly weighted against them" (1994, p. xv). This points to an ideal we might strive toward, and it illuminates as well a series of pitfalls and problems that must somehow be met and engaged. The ideal is knowledge, enlightenment, and truth on the one hand and, on the other, human freedom, emancipation, liberation for all, with emphasis on the dispossessed. That this core of humanism is unachievable in some ultimate or final form might be discouraging to some, but it does set a certain coherent standard within our existential boundaries and thus provides both focus and energy for our efforts.

Howard Zinn, the eminent historian and activist scholar who has written about these issues for decades, bemoans the honor, status, prestige, and pay academics garner "for producing the largest number of inconsequential studies in the history of civilization" (Zinn, 1997, p. 553). Zinn insists that we take note of and remember what motivated us to become teachers and scholars in the first place: we wanted to save lives, expand happiness, enable others to live more fully and freely. All of this is somehow rendered suspect in the insistent call for neutrality, objectivity, disinterested and discipline-based inquiry. His indictment: "Like politicians we have thrived on public innocence, with this difference: the politicians are paid for caring, when they really don't; we are paid for not caring, when we really do" (p. 553). Like Said, he is eager to resurrect the intellectual as engaged and caring, to close the "gap between the products of scholarly activity and the needs of a troubled world," to challenge the tenets of professional mythology, and to resist a situation where *we* publish while others perish.

Toward this end Zinn points out several commonplaces that undermine clear thought and humanistic judgment in all the intellectual precincts, from research project to academy to school to journal. These include the injunctions to carry on only "disinterested scholarship"; "be objective"; "stick to your discipline"; remember that "scientific" means "neutral"; and believe that there is no room in the world of ideas for something as suspect as passion, love, or emotions.

Zinn's refutation of these commandments begins with a defense of knowledge as a form of power, a particular kind of power that can be employed against the naked power of brute force. Knowledge has the power to undermine and, perhaps, to overthrow force. But to do so, knowledge must be freely sought, explicitly linked to moral purposes, and tied to conduct. It must stand for something.

Within our disputed spaces, objectivity is not a self-evident good. "If to be objective is to be scrupulously careful about reporting accurately what one sees," Zinn writes, "then of course, this is laudable" (Zinn, 1997, p. 504). If, for example, "objectivity" were to mean getting all the facts, data, and grounds one can, and making judgments in light of that, well, of course. But, Zinn points out, while a metal smith would be a fool to tinker or deceive in regard to accurate and reliable measurements, if "the metal smith has determined in advance that he prefers a plowshare [to a sword]," that determination in no way asks for distorted measurements. Just so a scholar: that she prefers peace to war, national sovereignty to occupation, and women's equality to patriarchy requires no distortion.

Calls for "balance" in teaching and scholarship, which draw force from a perceived tie to "objectivity," are similarly peculiar and precarious. If the purpose of education is to seek the truth through evidence and argument, "balance" could only sensibly mean this: find and present all the evidence you can. Very well. But if by "balance" people mean the equal presentation of contradictory perspectives, the classroom and the scholarly journal become little more than sites of incessant bickering. The classroom task, the obligation of the scholarly journal, is not quibbling, but achievement of judgment based on the widest and deepest available evidence. This means open debate, continuous inquiry, dialogue, *and* taking a stand. In reality, calls for "balance" are often in the service of a particular ideology.

If a historian speaks about Palestinian rights at Columbia University today, for example, the call goes up for "balance." If an Israeli diplomat defends Israeli policies at the same place, there is no comparable hue and cry.

Teachers must cultivate habits of vigilance and awareness, a radical openness, as we continually remind ourselves that in an infinite and expanding universe our ignorance is vast, and our finiteness itself is all the challenge we should need to propel ourselves forward. Knowing this, we nourish an imagination that's defiant and limitless and, like the color blue or love or friendship, impossible to define without a maiming reductiveness. The goal is discovery and surprise, and in the end it is our gusto, our immersion, our urgency, enthusiasm, and raw nerve that will take us hurtling toward the next horizon. We remind ourselves that the greatest work awaits us and that we are never higher than when we're not exactly certain where we're going.

We begin by recognizing that every human being, no matter who, is a gooey biological wonder, pulsing with the breath and beat of life itself, eating, sleeping, pissing and shitting, prodded by sexual urges, evolved and evolving, shaped by genetics, twisted and gnarled and hammered by the unique experiences of living. Every human being also has a unique and complex set of circumstances that makes his or her life understandable and sensible, bearable or unbearable. This recognition asks us to reject any action that treats anyone as an object, any gesture that *thingifies* human beings. It demands that we embrace the humanity of every student, and that we take their side.

Of course, there's always the possibility that we will be rejected for our ideas; there are certainly no guarantees that we will be rewarded. In fact, as each of us decides who to become as a teacher, we must practice choosing principle over the fearful calculus of pain and punishment. In the end we must decide how to live out our teaching lives in ways that refuse to make a mockery of our teaching values.

In Bertolt Brecht's play *Galileo* (1994), the great astronomer set forth into a world dominated by a mighty church and an authoritarian power. "The cities are narrow and so are the brains," he declared recklessly. Intoxicated with his own insights, Galileo found himself propelled toward revolution. Not only did his radical discoveries about the movement of the stars free them from the "crystal vault" that received truth insistently claimed fastened them to the sky, but his insights suggested something even more dangerous: that we, too, have embarked on a great voyage, that we are free and without the easy support that dogma provides. Here Galileo raised the stakes and risked taking on the establishment in the realm of its own authority, and it struck back fiercely. Forced to renounce his life's work under the exquisite pressure of the Inquisition, he denounced what he knew to be true and was welcomed back into the church and the ranks of the faithful, but exiled from humanity—by his own word. A former student later confronted him in the street: "Many on all sides followed you...believing that you stood, not only for a particular view of the movement of the stars, but even more for the liberty of teaching—in all fields. Not then for any particular thoughts, but for the right to think at all. Which is in dispute."

While there is no Galileo in the current dispute, this is surely what all the nonsense of demonizing and now excluding me finally comes down to: the right to a mind of one's own, the right to pursue an argument into uncharted spaces, the right to challenge the state or the church and its orthodoxy in the public square. The right to think at all.

REFERENCES

Brecht, B. (1994). *Galileo*. New York: Grove Press.

Said, E. (1994). *Representations of the intellectual*. New York: Vintage.

Zinn, H. (1997). *The Zinn reader: Writings on disobedience and democracy*. New York: Seven Stories.

CHAPTER NINE

Traveling Down a Desire Line

Surviving Where Academia and Community Meet[1]

JULIANNA ÁVILA

"I'm a wanderer from way back," I said to a colleague as we both left a meeting. We had been discussing my current position at the College of Liberal Arts and Science, where, from a tenure-track position in the English Department, I teach primarily English Education classes. A former high school teacher in Los Angeles, where I was raised, I went to graduate school at UC Berkeley, although there were many moves around the American West prior to that. Even though I am now near the opposite coast by choice, the parts of my career that I discuss in this chapter are the ones that have been unforeseen—the opportunities that initially seemed to be detours. I explore, in a non-chronological way, how traveling a desire line in academia, which is usually the most direct and/or easiest route between two points, has been a constructive, albeit non-linear, journey for me. I also question the assumption of linearity: Who defines what counts as "direct" or "easiest" in one's development as an academic? In attempting to balance professional (i.e., tenure) expectations and my own sense of responsibility as an educator living and working in sociocultural contexts, I have moved along a path that has been both rewarding and challenging. While a desire line usually strays from an official path in order to establish a more efficient route, much as travelers create shortcuts, my desire line has not necessarily been a more direct course to academic accomplishment. When I have experienced success, it has often been because I followed my own path and not the traditional one. In that way, what counts as "direct" and "easiest" has been relative since I had to redefine both while trying to do research and writing that would matter in academia and in the larger society. My "shortcuts" might well have lengthened my journey, although they also made it more meaningful.

Those shortcuts have also included a consideration, in constructing my academic life, of what it means to be a public scholar. While I publish in traditional academic venues, my attempt to be a public scholar includes working with marginalized and "minority" communities as often as I can. I do this because I grew up the daughter of a Latina mother and a White father, attending working-class schools in communities of diverse learners. Having received such a substantial education, I feel that I ought to offer the results of that education to individuals with cultural and socioeconomic backgrounds similar to those of my childhood peers.

The element of agency is crucial for me in that we, as scholars, should be able to rely upon some of our own parameters of what constitutes valuable work and not just labor to reinforce academic structures, or feel grateful to be employed in what is admittedly one tough job market. One bit of lore I heard from anxious fellow applicants when going onto the academic job market was that any one of us would be lucky to get a position, given the fierce competition. (The corollary of that assumption might well be that we should accept any job that we are offered.) I would counter that we need to advocate for ourselves and seek out positions that fit with our own definitions of what it means to be a public scholar. As I mentioned above, my own definition is focused on being able to study the relationships between students' literacies and social justice using methods that I feel are appropriate and fair (and not just publishable). I focus on the work itself and less on the outcomes, although I certainly have them in mind. First for me is doing work that I feel is important, and second is worrying about how it will advance my career.

I would hope that each of us could take our individual definitions of what it means to be a public scholar and negotiate how that will fit into, and balance with, our academic worlds. I also hope that the journey toward balance, rather than just fortune (as the saying goes), will favor the brave. In the following sections I describe how I have found—and am still finding—my own imperfect symmetry in an attempt to do scholarly research in a public realm.

STARTING THE JOURNEY: THE GOOD, THE BAD, THE IMMEDIATE

I moved, and still move, among diverse and sometimes divergent social, cultural, and economic worlds. Growing up, I felt that I was always just different enough to keep me from being totally accepted; of course, I do not know if this is how others perceived me, but it was nonetheless a powerful interpretation that prevented me from ever settling in. This agitation worked against me in graduate school, as I felt that I lacked some sort of necessary confidence and even a sense of entitlement that would position me to be successful; instead, I frequently dipped back into self-consciousness, a move that often silenced me. For example, I did not have a background that made graduate school seem like a given, and Berkeley seemed to be full of self-assured students. I never feel totally at ease in any given world, but that lack of comfort has made it easier for me to negotiate academia and balance its demands with my own desire to do work that has, in my view, some value outside of the university.

I sort of fell into publishing after graduation. During my first semester as an assistant professor, I wrote a book chapter—admittedly one of my easier forays into academic writing since it underwent editorial, rather than blind peer, review. I also wrote it about a project, described later in this chapter, that I cared so much about that the care overpowered my insecurity. Having two co-authors also allowed me to practice the production of academic discourse in my particular field without feeling entirely on my own. Despite my nagging self-consciousness, my voice came out because I felt passionate about the work I was describing.

Passion has been key for me, propelling me into doing the sort of research and writing that I cared about and then sustaining me through the droughts when I might find it difficult to complete or place a piece. If I were doing work whose primary purpose was to earn me credit in the academy, I would have quit not long after I started. While I did not take a class specifically on doing research one feels passionate about, it seemed to be an intrinsic part of what the people I admired included in their life's work.

In addition to passion, immediacy was relevant as I continued down this desire line in academia. When I went on to high school teaching soon after finishing my undergraduate degree, it was the immediacy of teaching and being a part of my students' lives, since I saw how their skepticism of, and struggles with, school literacy marginalized them and labeled them as "underachieving"; they were often the recipients of a remedial curriculum. Because I cared about those particular kids, I paid close attention to how school went for them and how they fared. When I felt that I did not have the necessary tools to help them alter their relationships with literacy, I went back to school. Their classroom lives, as well as what I did not know how to do as an educator, were in the forefront of my mind and motivated me to take on the intimidating world of graduate school. (If only I had known that it would seem safe and more navigable than academia as an assistant professor!) It was the combination of passion and immediacy that saw me through.

I often miss that immediacy, as academia so often seems to me to be about distance. All of my university and professional colleagues are busy with their own lives and research, and I rarely get to know my undergraduate and graduate students as I did my high school students and those I worked with in community settings. In my own life, a recent example of this would be doing a small study with junior high kids creating digital stories at ImaginOn, a children's library in

Charlotte, North Carolina. In the past, I would have done the teaching myself and studied it as a participant observer, but I felt that this approach had lacked rigor, especially since I had not videotaped similar past projects. So this time a librarian with interest and experience in digital storytelling did the teaching and most of the interaction with participants, while I took notes and interviewed them. I did feel better about the methods—doing it this way in this particular study—but wondered if the interviews would have had a different tone and depth had the participants known me as a teacher rather than just as a researcher. I find some irony in the fact that we spend years acquiring degrees that bring with them the seeming "promotion" of distance from those that we often worked with initially, and, in my case, those who had motivated me to pursue graduate study in the first place. It would be another group of learners, younger this time, that would motivate my scholarly work to this day.

A DESIRE LINE TO LOUISIANA

This part of my chapter recalls several pivotal moments for me, as I not only moved from being a graduate student to an assistant professor but also learned lessons that have helped me survive on my own terms in academia. It was an unlikely path and an unplanned research project. Because of my mother's death I had taken an additional year to finish writing my dissertation and, after making that decision, found out I had been awarded a fellowship that would provide some support during that final year. As a way to honor my mother's memory (since she and my father were the ones who first motivated and encouraged me to care about issues of social justice), I learned about work that Charles Underwood of UC Links and some of his Louisiana colleagues were doing with residents, including children, in Renaissance Village, the largest FEMA trailer park for Hurricane Katrina survivors. I describe this in a more scholarly way in a chapter that I co-authored (Ávila, Underwood, & Woodbridge, 2008), but suffice it to say that I figured that some of the children, many of whom had missed substantial amounts of schooling after the storm, could likely use what I had to offer—namely, my skills as an English and reading teacher. As part of a larger after-school program, I worked primarily with elementary-aged children to make digital stories and to write on a blog with donated laptops, learning the technology about one step ahead and then alongside them as they caught up and then overtook my skill set. They taught me and each other. And even though they could choose what to make their digital stories about, many chose to document the New Orleans and the lives they had been forced to leave behind.

In terms of a desire line, this Louisiana project was clearly located on one, and it seemed an unlikely detour. I had to *want* to be there, given how difficult the work was. However, despite the fact that it was so improbable, it served to teach me three important lessons. First, I was reminded of the fragility of collaboration. Many service providers were working in this makeshift place, and so to get anything done, we had to work together, something that—despite shared good intentions—required patience and constant work on my own communication skills. I was doing public work in a way I had not before, since I was not a part of a well-established organization such as a school. Being in a community very different from my own and certainly distinct from academia actually prepared me to function more constructively in academia, applying the same rules of collaboration I had worked to develop in Renaissance Village. (I was certainly not always successful at it, but I tried to learn from what I observed in myself and others, taking a kind of researcher reserve when there was conflict.) Second, there was that immediacy that I mentioned earlier in this chapter. I felt once again the responsibility of working with children and remembered why I cared about literacy education in the first place. Many of the children that I worked with seemed to travel a desire line of their own to learn digital storytelling (Ávila, 2008), and this subsequently inspired me in my work and life. It was also a timely reminder near the end of my time in graduate school of how important it is to work directly with learners. Third, and a lesson I would not come to appreciate until years after leaving this project, was the joy I felt at analyzing and writing about this work because it was not tied to anything formal. It was not part of my dissertation, and I did not have to try to publish it. I did this work because it moved me.

That I did go on to publish some of this work made me uncomfortable for a time, as it seemed I was profiting from describing others' hardships and sorrows. But the digital stories that the children made in Louisiana have served as a lesson to my university students in the ensuing years regarding the importance of story and self-expression (something we lose sight of in our standardized and assessment-driven educational culture) and the powerful creations that can come from putting digital tools in the hands of children who have often been underestimated. I have kept the website online with some of the children's digital stories because I made a promise to them that I would do so, and although it was a relatively small project, it has made a significant impact on me both as a teacher and a researcher. I do not know that it is particularly wise to start another project when one is finishing graduate school, but it was the work that unearthed a desire line for me, one which I have followed since.

DESIRE IN PLACE: FINDING A HOME IN ACADEMIA

The Renaissance Village project brought me back around to questioning the social and cultural contexts of schooling (public schooling in particular), and I again

wanted to focus on inequality in literacy education. Here again is where immediacy is useful, since it is difficult to see the effects of unequal opportunity and
remedial instructional approaches in students' lives and their developing literacy
identities and *not* want to address that in my own work. So the desire line then
turned to critical literacies (Ávila & Moore, 2012) and then, further on, to critical digital literacies (Ávila & Zacher Pandya, 2012a), which allowed me to again
bring in the digital tools I had been learning about since 2005. This critical literacies research was not what I had focused on in graduate school; rather, I had
arrived in a non-linear way. Another unplanned part of my own desire line has
been to include colleagues' articles and chapters in an edited journal issue (Ávila
& Zacher Pandya, 2012b) and two collections (Ávila & Zacher Pandya, 2012a;
Zacher Pandya & Ávila, 2013). While I did not intend to do this much editing
at the outset, it has been not just an academic exercise of editing but community
work of a different sort, immediate in its own particular way as we work to present
work and ideas to our part of the academic community.

What has been helpful for me is to think about my desire line as following
different directions along the way to being successful in the academy: I have to do
work that is multi-directional to meet tenure requirements; at the same time, my
own wish is to do work that serves a purpose in the larger society in which I live.
What this means for me is that not every research project I have done will result in
a publication for me. Others that did (or, I hope, will) result in publication might
not have had the sustained impact in the public schools or larger community
beyond the university that I would aim for, as I have had to make choices among
analysis, writing, editing, and development of future projects. Though I would
ideally like to do work that serves both worlds equally, the editing I have done,
for example, lacks the immediacy of working with middle and secondary school
learners. Because it is aimed at those in literacy and teacher education, however, it
is valuable to me in that regard. In some ways, this makes my intellectual life feel
like a multi-headed hydra monster, with heads facing several directions at once, a
potential logistical nightmare. But the alternative would be focusing on one part of
the path at the expense of another. So, again, it is a messy and non-linear journey,
to be sure. There are also times when my desire line forks in unexpected ways, and
I am unsure of which one to follow first. That is where and when instinct comes
into play, and I will go with my gut feeling, a most unscientific approach. In the
next section I focus on the issue of audience, a more straightforward subject.

AUDIENCE: FOR WHOM AM I PUBLISHING?

For me, the question of who will read my research and publications is a source of
ongoing tension. I always feel a debt to the students and learners that I study, and

although I know they will not be reading my work, I have them in mind when analyzing and writing. I earnestly try to pass on some of what I learn from them to other educators. I imagine that many of us do that, but finding the best venue in which to do that is where it gets tricky. Do I aim for a "top" journal so as to benefit my own career, or do I choose something that might be read more widely, such as an online journal? In my own academic job searches, I have gravitated toward universities where there is some latitude and choice when it comes to publication. During my development as a scholar I came to understand that I needed room to find the (seemingly magical) combination of what I could produce and what the scholarly community would accept as valid.

One way in which I have perhaps not been very mainstream in terms of educational research is that I do not, and likely will never, do quantitative research, and so I limit my potential audience in that regard. Although I had to learn the basics of it in graduate school, it has not made a significant appearance in my work. I sometimes suspect that if I included it in my methods, I would fare better in terms of grant work and publications. But it simply does not suit the sort of work I want to do, and so I accept the consequences of that part of my desire line. One way in which I have been surprised by this choice is the support I receive from colleagues in the humanities, an alliance that means much to me, since I consider myself first and foremost an English teacher. They are an audience who do not seem to mind that I am reluctant to conduct quantitative research of my own, and so I gain an unanticipated audience.

I have made peace with the tension of whom I am publishing for by trying both to meet tenure requirements and to acknowledge my responsibility to my research participants by writing for other scholars. I do sometimes fear that I am spending a great deal of time writing for just a few. However, achieving success in the academy, an important part of which is certainly the peer-reviewed publication process, means that I can continue to do the work I think has some social import. I also negotiate this tension by sharing what I do with my own students; they are an important audience for me, although one that is not necessarily officially recognized. Once a piece is accepted, I do not know who will read it, or to what end. Thus, although I am writing for my colleagues and attempting to join professional communities, I am also writing for the more immediate audience of my students, though not necessarily in a traditional way. It is perhaps due to my self-consciousness as an academic, or my feeling that I was not groomed for this professional life, that I rarely assign my own work in my classes. Instead, I share the ideas and insights from my research and writing in class activities. That is one of my ways of honoring those I study: as a traveler I view this as bringing the lessons of one landscape to another.

I continue to strive for balance when it comes to doing work that matters in academia and work that matters in community (as I define it). Being on a desire line means that I am unsure of how the journey will progress, but I am confident that it may well not be the easiest or most direct route along the way.

NOTE

1. I would like to dedicate this chapter to Charles Underwood, my example of the very best that a public scholar can be.

REFERENCES

Ávila, J. (2008). A desire path to digital storytelling. *Teachers College Record*. http://www.tcrecord.org. ID Number: 15463.

Ávila, J., & Moore, M.T. (2012). Critical literacy, digital literacies and Common Core Standards: A workable union? *Theory into Practice*, *51*(1), 27–33.

Ávila, J., Underwood, C., & Woodbridge, S. (2008). "I'm the expert now": Digital storytelling and transforming literacies among displaced children. In D. McInerney & A.D. Liem (Eds.), *Research on sociocultural influences on motivation and learning: Teaching and learning: International best practice* (Vol. 8). Charlotte, NC: Information Age Publishing.

Ávila, J., & Zacher Pandya, J. (Eds.). (2012a). *Critical digital literacies as social praxis: Intersections and challenges*. New York: Peter Lang.

Ávila, J., & Zacher Pandya, J. (2012b). Guest-editing a volume of *Theory into Practice: The future of critical literacies in US schools*, *51*(1).

Zacher Pandya, J., & Ávila, J. (Eds.). (2013). *A new look at critical literacies: Theories and practices across contexts*. New York: Routledge.

CHAPTER TEN

Conversations That Matter

Community-Based Practice in Support of the Public Good

ALAN TINKLER AND BARRI TINKLER

INTRODUCTION

There are conversations that matter for public intellectuals. For us, as educators who prepare teachers, those conversations advance equitable and appropriate learning opportunities for youth as they prepare for meaningful lifelong journeys. Our story offers an example of two public intellectuals who engage in community-based research and teaching for the public good. To put this in a slightly different way, as public intellectuals, we remain committed to (re)claiming the dialogue in education in a way that supports consequential conversations around practice and policy, particularly those conversations informed by the needs of the local community.

Our local United Way has identified education (to achieve potential), income (to promote financial stability), and health (to promote well-being) as three "Building Blocks for a Good Quality of Life" following a series of community conversations. Since impact is central to the United Way's mission of "improving people's lives…by pursuing real social change through collective community strategies" (United Way of Chittenden County, n.d.), it comes as no surprise that these community-determined goals are used when making funding decisions. Impact is also salient when we think about the mission of the University of Vermont (UVM), where we work. However, faculty impact is traditionally assessed based on how publications are received by the academy rather than on the impact faculty work has within the local community. Our work as scholars seeks to address this disparity by offering examples of how faculty can work together with communities, both local and academic, to advance social justice through community-based scholarship and action that is meaningful to the communities with which we work.

For us, scholarship, action, and impact are intertwined and begin with community-based conversations. Alphonso Lingis (2007), an American philosopher who has written extensively about the relationship of the self to the community, highlights the connection between discourse and action: "Words order our action: they organize our environment.... Our words are not only indicative or informative but also imperative: they launch and command our action or inaction" (p. 28). While this does not necessarily call for a paradigmatic shift, it does locate action as central to the process of developing public knowledge through discourse. For us this translates into the notion that developing public knowledge and understanding should relate directly to inclusion, action, and impact. This is particularly important given that, as Lingis (2007) writes in an essay titled "Professional Dishonor," "[t]he established discourse and the code of professional conduct can limit and even dislodge our experience of what is important and urgent.... We can find that the established discourse takes over our voice and orders our actions" (p. 123). As public intellectuals, it remains crucial to maintain our voice, a voice that (as Lingis notes) is too often lost within established discourses. For us, the imperative is to advance social justice, and in order to do this, an engaged code of conduct must be central to the role of public intellectuals.

In this chapter we describe our ongoing efforts to make connections and facilitate conversations between the academic institution where we work and the community in which it is situated. As we tell our story, we hope the following concepts will resonate: (1) the need for social justice to be a guiding principle when thinking about educational opportunity, (2) the central role of action and impact, and (3) the merit of community-based knowledge and practice. In the end, our hope is to provide a lens to understand how and why it is important for academics (as public intellectuals) to engage with their communities to bridge the divide between academia and the community in order to advance opportunities for youth and their families.

Social Justice as a Guiding Principle for Our Work

We began our work together as Peace Corps volunteers in Papua New Guinea, where we served for 2 years as teachers at a regional boarding school for students in grades 7–10. Results of exams administered to grade 10 students determined which ones would return to their villages and which would continue to provincial high schools for grades 11 and 12. We met during the initial training for our group, and after our first year of service, the deputy registrar general of Papua New Guinea officiated at our wedding ceremony in Port Moresby. Among the many lessons that we learned while abroad, one that stuck with us was the importance of local knowledge and understanding, since our students came from five language groups (in a country where there are over 800 indigenous languages). To navigate our school community, we had to be sensitive to conversations from all of the language communities that sent students to the school as well as the communities that bordered our school. We also had to prepare those students who would be matriculating to provincial boarding schools. Though we had concerns about an educational system that offered opportunities for only the highest achievers, we had to work within that system. Not surprisingly, these institutional structures impacted our work with the school community as well as the surrounding community.

In her superb book *Unequal Childhoods: Class, Race, and Family Life*, Annette Lareau (2011) begins her second chapter with a quotation from C. Wright Mills: "The life of an individual cannot be adequately understood without references to the institutions within which his biography is enacted" (p. 14). This idea offers a constructive frame because it affirms the importance of institutions as we examine biographies. Such a focus on institutions also offers an opportunity to explore, through a critical lens, the relative stability of the status quo and what is necessary to effect change. In many important ways, this thinking aligns with the critical pedagogy of Paulo Freire. In *Pedagogy of the Oppressed*, for instance, Freire (2011) writes: "Knowledge emerges only through invention and re-invention, through the restless, impatient, continuing, hopeful inquiry human beings pursue in the world, with the world, and with each other" (p. 72). For the authors, it is this inquiry that guides our work to advance social justice and address systemic oppression. It is an inquiry that requires constant collaboration and cooperation. In other words, knowledge and understanding are insufficient, as we must seek ways to engage in ongoing evaluation and action to ensure that practices emerge to meet the changing needs of individuals and communities within a dynamic world.

This includes coming to terms with social justice, which, according to the *Oxford English Dictionary* (Social Justice, n.d.), has been a phrase that has been used since the nineteenth century, primarily in politics and philosophy, and means "justice at the level of a society or state as regards the possession of wealth, commodities, opportunities, and privileges." The entry notes that "[m]uch of the debate surrounding social justice has been concerned with the precise nature of fair distribution, and to what extent this may conflict with individual rights of acquisition and ownership." While material goods play a role, there is more at stake, since opportunities and privileges are incorporated into the definition. To that end, some innovative economists such as Martha Nussbaum and Amartya Sen have focused their attention on opportunities and capabilities. In fact, Nussbaum and Sen (2009) "have concluded that the whole utilitarian approach should be rejected—to be replaced, perhaps, by an account of the many different kinds of activity that actually make up a 'thriving' human life" (p. 2). Social justice, in other words, is aligned with equitable opportunity to advance capabilities for everyone to thrive. This is a reasonable way to state the goal of public intellectuals concerned with advancing social justice; not surprisingly, it also echoes the goal of our local United Way chapter.

Since our role at the University of Vermont is to prepare teachers, our primary responsibility is to support the advancement and development of teaching professionals. As part of our work, we also have to be mindful of the barriers to professional development. This means that the local matters both in concept and in practice as our students develop their professional knowledge and proficiencies. While focusing on knowledge, skills, and disposition, we are mindful of both the school environment and the community environment. One way to frame this is that both school and society matter when thinking about engaging educational opportunities for community youth. One reason we moved to Vermont relates to the state's governance structure. Vermont is committed to local control. Town Meeting Day is both a myth and a practice across Vermont. With respect to schools, Vermont is notorious for its number of school boards. Rumor has it that in Vermont there are more school board members than English teachers (because in many districts there is both a local board and a supervisory union board, making some schools subject to the decision-making authority of two school boards). Vermont, though, has a strong commitment to K–12 education and innovative practice. For instance, Vermont recently passed Act 77, an education act that promotes personalized learning plans for all students working toward a diploma that can be awarded based on proficiencies rather than the prototypical counting of seat units (such as 4 years of English and 2 years of a foreign language). All of these factors, which are unique to Vermont, impact how we as public intellectuals work to prepare teaching professionals through a social justice lens.

Our Efforts to Pursue Action and Impact

In our current role as faculty at the University of Vermont, we teach in the Department of Education's Secondary Education Program and have worked to develop a strong foundation of community-based service-learning experiences to build on our commitment to advancing social justice. Our scholarship, in fact, has focused on trying to understand best practices for this community-based pedagogy that provides meaningful learning opportunities for students as well as service to local community partners. The purpose of this work is twofold: first, to develop knowledge and understanding of the local community in which we place our teacher education candidates, and second, akin to the intent behind the work of Paulo Freire (2011), to act. Through action (say, working on a problem of common concern such as poverty), we seek to contribute to public knowledge as the foundation for the public good, a public good where policies and practices work to advance education, income, and health for all members of the community. To be clear, the opportunity to effect change is directly related to the ability to disseminate why changes in practice are important to advance social justice. In many ways, the United Way has provided a model of how to do this by forming impact teams around education, health, and income. As mentioned earlier, the impact teams are charged with making distribution decisions and advancing understanding about the local context and needs. Because the United Way fully recognizes that the community is a dynamic and complex system, it is committed to promoting continuous improvement.

In order to account for the complexity of our community, we have integrated service-learning experiences into our courses to support service opportunities in line with identified community needs. One example is the ongoing service-learning partnerships Alan has developed to support his secondary literacy methods course. Each semester, Alan's students provide tutoring at several local community centers. This tutoring supports the academic achievement of local students who are English language learners (Burlington is a refugee relocation community) as well as students dealing with generational poverty. The partnership also benefits the university students who acquire an understanding of instructional strategies for working with English language learners as well as developing a more complex understanding of literacy within and across academic disciplines. Barri has recently developed a service-learning partnership with Serve Burlington, an organization that provides citizenship test preparation classes for adult immigrants and refugees. Barri's social studies methods class is adapting the course curriculum to meet the needs of students at various levels of English proficiency. Students in the course will also provide tutoring support during the citizenship class sessions.

In addition to working with community partners to advance our teacher preparation program goals, we have been involved with a high school reform conversation (called the Partnership for Change) funded by the Nellie Mae Foundation. In fact, during the Partnership for Change's first year, Alan was a co-coordinator for the initiative along with Peter McConville, a teacher at Burlington High School. (With the progress made during the first year, we were able to hire Hal Colston as the initiative's current director.) The Partnership for Change was conceptualized and initiated by way of a community participatory process that designed the initiative around five strategic areas: (1) Student Leadership and Engagement, (2) Community-Based Learning, (3) Family-School Partnerships, (4) Proficiency-Based Learning, and (5) Teaching and Learning Environments (Partnership for Change, n.d.). Each strategic area is supported by a research fellow who examines local and national practices and an implementation team comprised of local stakeholders, including students, teachers, parents, and community members (including faculty from some of the local colleges and universities). The

Partnership for Change's goal is to remodel the educational opportunities for local youth, including refugees and students living in poverty, to ensure that all youth are fully prepared for the future in a world where critical thinking, collaboration, creativity, and problem solving are necessary for success.

As part of the remodeling effort, the Partnership for Change is promoting community conversations to understand what skills and dispositions students should have upon graduation, while at the same time supporting innovative practices around teaching and learning. Not surprisingly, the Partnership for Change supports multiple measures to examine the efficacy of the remodeling effort. The use of multiple measures (for program evaluation) reminds us that it is important to use multiple measures when assessing students. Reflecting back on our Peace Corps experience, there were a number of talented students who were not able to proceed to grade 11 based solely on their grade 10 exam scores.

The use of an ecological lens to examine reform initiatives was the focus of a recent presentation we delivered at the American Association for Teaching and Curriculum (AATC) conference in Chicago. The presentation was formed around ideas in an essay, "Pathways to Understanding: Using an Ecological Lens to Assess a School Reform Initiative" (Tinkler & Tinkler, 2014), which argues that "resilient systems are complex and diverse, and they adapt to shocks as well as opportunities since resilience is the concept that recognizes how healthy systems change and develop through time" (p. 2). This critical lens recognizes the complexity of systems and the temporal nature of systems, an approach that clearly aligns with the United Way's framework and its commitment to continuous improvement. As public intellectuals, we relish the inquiry process that allows us a chance to be part of the conversation to develop community-based knowledge and practice. For us, this means that we are also committed to collaboration, and for us this means emphasizing the importance of cooperation, because cooperation focuses attention not only on the decision-making process but also on the results. Our commitment to cooperation, we believe, advances social justice.

Joshua Greene (2013a), a contemporary philosopher with a deep understanding of cognitive psychology, argues that "morality evolved to enable cooperation" (p. 23). Greene recognizes that there are "different ways of being cooperative" (2013b, para. 7), which means that there are "different ways of solving that problem" (2013b, para. 7). In fact, he suggests that "[s]olving a problem is often a matter of framing it in the right way" (2013a, p. 349). When presenting this framework in his book *Moral Tribes: Emotion, Reason, and the Gap Between Us and Them* (2013a), Greene compares the individualistic and communalistic perspectives. He recognizes that moral frameworks allow either approach to solve problems. Complications arise, however, when groups with different values need to cooperate to solve a problem. The solution, though, is in hand, because we are able to understand our decision-making process, allowing us to frame questions that allow us to find solutions. In other words, the individualistic approach (which aligns with conservative philosophy) and the collectivist approach (which aligns with liberal philosophy) can achieve consensus, particularly if partisan positioning is avoided. Building consensus (building cooperation), however, often relies on a willingness to fully know and understand another's perspective.

Our Focus on Community-Based Knowledge and Practice

Valuing the knowledge and perspectives of community members frames our work, since it is by understanding our community that we are able to support opportunities and develop capabilities (both for individuals and for the community). When writing a Learn and Service America grant application in the spring of 2010 (with the goal of advancing service-learning opportunities across the teacher preparation programs), we incorporated a community-based participatory process to discern the best way to roll out service-learning opportunities for our teacher education students. The participatory process allowed us to frame our work to attend to the needs of both refugees and youth experiencing generational poverty. One intentional goal, like a goal of the United Way, was to use community conversations to advance public knowledge and understanding with attention to individual and community strengths.

As part of our process, we collaborated with community partners to identify best practices for our community. To this end, we have engaged in a number of conversations to discern effective practices among various stakeholders, including the University of Vermont's Community-University Partnerships and Service-Learning Office. With respect to Alan's literacy class, where his students have been involved with academic support for youth at three community centers, Alan has worked closely with community partners—specifically Gabe Tufo-Strouse from the King Street Center and Ethan Hausman from the O'Brien Community Center—to establish best practices. This collaborative work has resulted in an essay, "Six Things Community Partners Want You to Know About Service-Learning," which includes Gabe and Ethan as coauthors (Tinkler, Tinkler, Hausman, & Tufo-Strouse, 2013). As the title makes clear, the piece articulates best practices from the community partner perspective. The essay has also provided a local context for us as we continue to develop other service-learning relationships.

In addition to co-authoring the manuscript, Alan and Ethan attended the International Center for Service-Learning in Teacher Education (ICSLTE) conference at Duke University, where they presented the paper. At the conference, the University of Vermont's teacher education program was recognized (Honorable Mention: Service-Learning Excellence in Teacher Education) for work done to advance understanding around service-learning practice and impact. Alan and Ethan also had a chance to engage other community scholars from across the globe. This discovery process enabled us to make some meaningful changes to our partnership. One was an increased awareness about how important recognition is to advance the work. To this end, we have been mindful of finding opportunities to showcase the work being done at O'Brien's academic assistance center. The center recently hired an academic assistance coordinator, and this position came about because the community recognized the important work being done to support local youth.

Attending the conference confirmed another aspect of our work. In addition to collaborating and cooperating with local stakeholders, the ongoing national and international conversations are important, since our efforts are informed by the work done by other scholars and public intellectuals. At the national level, we are members of the Service-Learning Special Interest Group of the American Educational Research Association (AERA), the premier venue for the dissemination of educational research. This special-interest group disseminates research nationally while valuing the local knowledge acquired through service-learning pedagogy. Increasingly, researchers are recognizing the importance of the local context. In other words, there is greater cooperation within and across communities. Bryk, Gomez, and Grunow (2010), of the Carnegie Foundation for the Advancement of Teaching, acknowledged this need in their *Getting Ideas into Action: Building Networked Improvement Communities in Education*. They argue for "new arrangements for disciplined inquiry where the work of research and practice join a more dynamic and interactive fashion" (p. 4). By establishing networks around a common goal (in their essay, Bryk and colleagues focus on improving math literacy), stakeholders are able to advance practice through a reinforced understanding that the local context matters a great deal. A more thoughtful understanding of the local context allows us to ask the right questions. When thinking about poverty, for instance, Mark Rank (2005) provides a powerful analysis regarding poverty, specifically: (1) "poverty results from structural failings" (p. 176), and (2) "poverty constitutes deprivation" (p. 181). When this understanding is part of the community-based knowledge, the community is able to work to find solutions that are context specific.

Central to the process of seeking solutions are public intellectuals who engage with these conversations with a focus toward cooperation. Another useful way to think about this is through the lens of effective critical thinking. In *Pedagogy of Freedom: Ethics, Democracy, and Civic Courage*, Paulo Freire (1998) spends time reflecting on critical thinking, and he finds that "[t]hinking correctly is, in other words, not an isolated act or something to draw near in isolation but an act of communication" (p. 42). From our perspective, to think correctly means developing community-based knowledge and practice that supports and expands the opportunities and capabilities for all community members. Central to public knowledge (and dialogue) is the recognition that our emerging understanding allows us to advance social justice. Put another way, our view is that public intellectuals are equally committed to understanding and action, since desire without action is, quite simply, not enough.

Conclusion: The Role of the Public Intellectual

We view our roles as public intellectuals in line with developing community-based knowledge and practice; we believe, in other words, that the role of the public intellectual is to advocate for and to be part of a process that looks into ways to enhance capabilities and opportunities across the community. What this also means is that as public intellectuals we speak as part of a community, and the manner of our speech is important. Let us return to Alphonso Lingis, who thinks and writes about what it means to connect to each other. When breaking this down in terms of speech, Lingus (1998) finds: "When we speak, we speak to others. Whatever we say, we say in response to what another asks or has asked. Whatever we say we put forth for her assent, her sanction, her interpretation, her judgment. To agree to speak, already to answer his greeting, is to have already accepted the other as our judge" (p. 136). For us as public intellectuals, this means that we have a responsibility to our community, which stands in judgment of our actions, including our research and the questions that guide our research. It means, too, that we cannot find solitude in the fortress of the academy.

In no small way, the (re)claiming of the public dialogue is a necessary response to systemic inequalities and the suffering caused by inadequate access to health care, sufficient income, and quality education. Henry Giroux (2012) uses Paulo Freire to frame his thinking around intellectuals:

> Vigilant in bearing witness to the individual and collective suffering of others, Paulo shunned the role of the isolated intellectual as an existential hero who struggles alone. He believed that intellectuals must respond to the call for making the pedagogical more political with a continuing effort to build coalitions, affiliations, and social movements capable of mobilizing real power and promoting substantive social change. (Giroux, 2012, pp. 122–123)

In our view, this sums up nicely the role of the public intellectual. Public intellectuals seek to empower and promote substantive change in the company of others.

REFERENCES

Bryk, A.S., Gomez, L.M., & Grunow, A. (2010). *Getting ideas into action: Building networked improvement communities in education.* Stanford, CA: Carnegie Foundation for the Advancement of Teaching. Available at http://www.carnegiefoundation.org/sites/default/files/bryk-gomez_building-nics-education.pdf

Freire, P. (1998). *Pedagogy of freedom: Ethics, democracy, and civic courage*. New York: Rowman & Littlefield.

Freire, P. (2011). *Pedagogy of the oppressed* (30th anniversary ed.). New York: Continuum.

Giroux, H. (2012). *Education and the crisis of public values: Challenging the assault on teachers, students, & public education*. New York: Peter Lang.

Greene, J. (2013a). *Moral tribes: Emotion, reason, and the gap between us and them*. New York: Penguin.

Greene, J. (2013b). *Deep pragmatism* [video transcript]. Retrieved from The Edge website at http://edge.org/conversation/deep-pragmatism

Lareau, A. (2011). *Unequal childhoods: Class, race, and family life* (2nd ed.). Berkeley: University of California Press.

Lingis, A. (1998). *The imperative*. Bloomington: Indiana University Press.

Lingis, A. (2007). *The first person singular*. Evanston, IL: Northwestern University Press.

Nussbaum, M., & Sen, A. (2009). *The quality of life*. Oxford, UK: Oxford University Press.

Partnership for Change. (n.d.). *Implementation teams*. Retrieved February 8, 2013 from http://partnershipvt.org/approach/implementation-teams/

Rank, M. (2005). *One nation, underprivileged: Why American poverty affects us all*. Oxford, UK: Oxford University Press.

Social Justice [Def. 1]. (n.d.). In *Oxford English dictionary online*. Retrieved November 14, 2013, from http://www.oed.com/socialjustice

Tinkler, A., & Tinkler, B. (2014). Pathways to understanding: Using an ecological lens to assess a school reform initiative. Manuscript in preparation.

Tinkler, A., Tinkler, B., Hausman, E., & Tufo-Strouse, G. (2013). Six things community partners want you to know about service-learning. Manuscript submitted for publication.

United Way of Chittenden County [Vermont]. (n.d.). *Mission*. Retrieved from http://www.unitedwaycc.org/about-us/our-mission-and-work/

CHAPTER ELEVEN

An Inevitable Dichotomy…*Really*?

Harmonizing Public Intellectual Work *with* Academic Work

STEVEN JAY GROSS

In 1993 I taught a senior seminar at Trinity College of Vermont and assigned *Postmodern Education* by Aronowitz and Giroux (1991). That's where I first came across the term "public intellectual." Inspired by that concept, I immediately challenged my students to think of themselves as educators writ large with civic responsibilities beyond the classroom. I felt that at Trinity this idea had a serious chance, since our college was dedicated to social justice. To say the least, it was a hard sell. Paralleling the dilemma facing many academics, my students felt that public intellectual work would take them away from their primary duties as newly minted classroom teachers, perhaps causing unnecessary problems with their school's administration. My point that public intellectual work and academic work were mutually supporting simply didn't make sense to them.

I was puzzled. The term "public intellectual" may have been new to me, but the behavior had been part of my professional life since the mid-1970s. I was then a social studies teacher at the Philadelphia YMCA's Penn Center Academy, but I also served as the education coordinator for a Chinatown community organization. I believed my time teaching English language and citizenship classes was just as important as my high school teaching job. Both involved working with people needing to move on in their lives, and both were rewarding.

In the early 1980s I experienced what I call a 5-year hiatus from education and went into my family's furniture business. We imported modern furniture from around the world and ran four large retail stores as well as the commercial furniture division that I led. This was during the Reagan-era military buildup. I joined a group of other business people who were deeply concerned with the macho saber rattling coming from Washington. Our group, Business Executives for Nuclear Arms Control (BENAC), emphasized negotiated reductions in weaponry rather than pushing the other side to the brink. I was a steering committee member and head of the education committee. This was a public intellectual exercise, and it helped my time in business to seem more valuable. It also elevated the profile of our business in the wider community. Yet my work in BENAC never scored any points for me with other members of our firm who saw my participation as extraneous to the task of selling more furniture.

In 1986 I left the furniture business and city life to move my family to a cabin in Vermont's Green Mountains and move myself back into education as a curriculum and staff development director for the Rutland Northeast Supervisory Union. I quickly learned that titles and bureaucratic culture had little importance in a state where everyone—from the shopkeepers to the governor—was on a first-name basis. Just as amazing to a person coming from a big city, everyone seemed to know everyone else. I learned that a state could be one large community and that I could have a useful role to play. In this beautiful rural world, educational work was directly tied to the life of the community.

The Vermont culture of community, added to my earlier experience, established a pattern that would both help and challenge me in the years ahead. As chief of curriculum and instruction for the State of Vermont, for example, I was responsible for a project called the Vermont Common Core of Learning. Diametrically opposed to today's Common Core State Standards, our effort started by coming to the people of our state with what amounted to a tabula rasa. We believed that the public schools were given that name because they belonged to the people and that the people of our state had the right to set our curricular goals. So we held over 50 forums around the state that included over five thousand community members. In some cases, people came to the forums in blizzard conditions, not just to help the state's Department of Education, but also to have a voice in setting local education priorities. At the end of one forum, a mom looked around the room at her fellow townspeople and said, "I am not a rich person, and I may have been quiet until today, but let me tell all of you, I won't be quiet anymore!" Once again, connecting the public to our academic work led to better results and seemed a natural combination. Yet there were detractors who wanted to shut down our community outreach.

In 1993 I joined the faculty at Trinity College of Vermont. Given what I had done up to that point, it's not surprising that I made such a big deal about being a public intellectual. I simply did not see much of a division between teaching and scholarship on the one hand and joining in public dialogue about education issues on the other. However, as my department chair, Steve Garger, strongly advised, learning to be a professor takes years. So I spent much of my 6 years at Trinity learning to work effectively with a wide variety of students in classroom teaching, advising, supervising student teacher placements, and making professional conference presentations. Consequently, my time as a public intellectual was somewhat limited.

At Steve's suggestion, I pursued publication of my first book, a long-time dream of mine. I remember the telephone call to Ron Brandt, then executive editor for the Association of Supervision and Curriculum Development (ASCD) in which I shared the kernel of an idea for a book on curriculum leadership. I spent the next year working on proposals, getting feedback, and re-drafting. Finally, I got the contract and went to work investigating successful curriculum innovations in the United States and Canada. While one of my colleagues accused me of jet-setting because of my research travels, leaders at Trinity smiled on my work and gave me much-needed research grants. At our small liberal arts college, writing a book of this kind was valued, and I was respected as a budding scholar.

Writing for a publisher like ASCD could be considered an act of public intellectual scholarship, since the organization's membership is largely school faculty and administrators, not university faculty and researchers. Undoubtedly my book *Staying Centered: Curriculum Leadership in a Turbulent Era* has been read by field educators. Yet it has also been used as a course text. So, it is not clear to me exactly where the line between public intellectual writing starts and ends. This is a major issue for those of us who cross boundaries, because we need to define ourselves as scholars in the academy while still doing the work that means so much to us.

Something happened to me as a result of writing *Staying Centered*. I became fascinated with research and writing. The more I did, the more I wanted to do. Investigating schools and districts trying to initiate and sustain deep innovation was a rewarding challenge and highly relevant to improving public education. This led me to a job search for a position at a research university. Amazingly, I found just such an opportunity at my alma mater, Temple University. My career came full circle in 1999 when I joined the Educational Administration program there as an un-tenured associate professor.

The priorities of this new place were made clear to me at once. The search committee was friendly but straightforward when they advised me to start steering my writing away from practitioner publications and toward a more academic audience. As an associate professor, my tenure clock was short. I had about 18 months to turn my writing and research to this new task. This was harder than I anticipated, but with helpful advice from colleagues and a writing schedule that often started at 7:30 a.m. and ended at 11:00 p.m., I found my way. Peer-reviewed journals articles and chapters in scholarly books became the order of the day, as did presentations at national and international academic conferences.

While I did not stop presenting at practitioner conferences, I gradually realized that this had to be above and beyond institutionally recognized work. This was not a surprise, because it fit the pattern that I found in my field research. Innovative schools and districts likewise had to do everything that everyone else was doing and do their innovation as an extra. My professional life started to parallel the organizations I studied. So I wrote for academic audiences but also served as the executive editor for ASCD's Curriculum Handbook. I weathered unfriendly letters from one administrator warning me that I needed to publish more in peer-reviewed journals. Trusted colleagues reminded me that such notices were as inaccurate as they were common. Their analysis of my productivity during the pre-tenure period was crucial because it gave me courage.

My department chair, Joan Shapiro, was a superb mentor. I think one illustration will give the reader an idea of how critical her guidance was to me. As anyone connected with the academy knows, one's curriculum vitae is a crucial document because it describes in great detail productivity in the areas of scholarship, teaching, and service. This was hardly news to me when I arrived at Temple University. What I didn't realize was the extent to which each of us was expected to detail and claim credit for our work. This flew in the face of how I was raised, namely, to do my best to contribute and not look for external praise. Joan quickly realized that I was selling myself short in a dangerous way. If everyone else being considered for tenure carefully listed every accomplishment and I simply glossed over mine, I would appear to be unproductive rather than modest. One day, I walked into her office with the nth version of my vitae for her consideration. She read it carefully and handed it back to me with advice on how to improve it with more detail. I said something like, "This is stupid and I feel like a braggart. I won't write another word!" Joan looked at me, pointed to her office door and said, "Steve, march out of here, go to your office, and hand me the revised vitae by the end of the day." I did it and it worked. This is only a small example of an ethic of care shown to me by Joan. I am convinced that any of us who are drawn to being public intellectuals need just this kind of support if we are to survive and thrive in our institutions.

Once I earned tenure, I felt free to make more connections with the wider world. One day I was having lunch with Bill Mathis, then superintendent of the Rutland Northeast Supervisory Union. He mentioned a new group that was forming called the Vermont Society for the Study of Education (VSSE) and asked if I wanted to come along. I joined Bill, Susan Ohanian, and Sid Glassner as a senior fellow. Through writing, publishing, conferences, and direct appeals to policymakers, we made a strong case against the excesses of the accountability movement that was just then gaining momentum. We were one of the first groups in the nation to work against No Child Left Behind, because we felt it would lead to a fixation on punitive testing, a narrowed curriculum, and a micromanagement of schools and teachers by distant bureaucrats. In my opinion, time and the weight of evidence have proven this to be the case.

ORGANIZING THE NEW DEEL

Despite our efforts in VSSE, it was clear by the early 2000s that extreme forms of accountability, coupled with a push toward market forces and privatization, were ascendant—not only in the United States but around the world. I was starting on a sabbatical leave in the summer of 2004 when national policies I could not accept kept me from calmly pursuing the neutral research agenda. NCLB had become truly destructive and was leading many of the nation's teachers and school leaders to knuckle under to that law's threats of punishment. Worse, I found too many accounts of children losing valuable time that could have been spent on creative learning but was instead wasted on meaningless test preparation.

I felt that we had to do something as a community of education scholars. I was inspired by the example of the democratic administration movement of the 1930s and 1940s (Koopman, Miel, & Misner, 1943). Facing the threat of Nazi Germany, imperial Japan, and fascist Italy, our predecessors decided that the answer to a dangerous world was more democracy in America's public schools. In the post-9/11 world, with our nation engaged in two wars, that example seemed apt.

Walking toward Middlebury College's library, I picked up my cell phone and called Joan Shapiro. "Joan, I am calling to let you know that I will never again help our students become cogs in some accountability machine." After a brief pause, Joan reminded me that, to her knowledge, I actually never did help anyone become a cog in any accountability machine. Then she asked me what this was all about. I explained my idea—namely, that we start to organize our generation of educational leaders with an updated version of the democratic administration movement. Again, there was a pause. Then Joan replied, "If you add ethics to democracy, I'm in."

That is how she and I decided to start a movement based on democracy and ethics in educational leadership we call the New DEEL (Democratic Ethical Educational Leadership). We pulled together some initial ideas and quickly thought of ways to link with others around the world. Our first connection was at that fall's Values and Leadership conference held in Barbados. This group, closely affiliated with our learned society, the University Council for Educational Administration (UCEA), meets annually to share new research and theory on ethics in educational leadership. During the conference we presented our concerns and our suggestion for organizing the New DEEL. The positive reception we received set in motion the process of finding allies and gaining a sense of direction. Thanks to the support of Executive Director Michelle Young of UCEA, we were able to make a presentation at that year's annual UCEA conference. We followed up with two winter strategy sessions held at Temple University, where colleagues from around the United States and Canada met. At the first such meeting, a colleague from the University of Vermont, Judith Aiken, was critical in helping us craft our mission statement:

> The mission of the New DEEL is to create an action-oriented partnership, dedicated to inquiry into the nature and practice of democratic, ethical educational leadership through sustained processes of open dialogue, right to voice, community inclusion, and responsible participation toward the common good. We strive to create an environment to facilitate democratic ethical decision-making in educational theory and practice which acts in the best interest of all students. (Gross & Shapiro, 2005)

Crucial to the New DEEL is our insistence that leadership is broadly defined to include teachers, students, families, and community members along with the traditional administrative leaders. We do not accept the traditional view that public intellectual work is antithetical to serious scholarship. In fact, we see these as mutually supporting pursuits. From the start we outlined crucial areas of development, including publishing and research, as well as curriculum planning in educational administration programs. Through the development of new courses, publishing, and conferences, we have built a community of like-minded colleagues in the United States, Canada, Australia, New Zealand, the UK, Sweden, Jamaica, and Hong Kong from over 30 universities and school districts.

At Temple University, we teach a graduate course called Profiles of Democratic Ethical Leadership. Students study leaders such as Ella Flagg Young, Cesar Chavez, Desmond Tutu, and John Dewey as they faced life-defining critical incidents. Using Jerome Bruner's Concept Attainment model, the class builds a definition inductively from week to week as we see the common qualities that these past and present leaders exhibit. Students then reflect on ways these exemplars can help today's practitioners face current challenges. Other courses in ethics and organizational development have been modified to expose students to our New DEEL approach to today's education policy, and our principalship certification program is infused with this same point of view. In all cases, we are dedicated to the idea that students need to thrive in their current positions while they work with others to change policy directions. Similar course development is occurring in other universities with New DEEL members. It is also worth noting that many master's and doctoral students tell us that they come to our programs because we have taken a stand and that we have a clear perspective.

Also contradicting the notion that public intellectual work is at odds with scholarship, New DEEL faculty members have published widely over the past decade in books, journal articles, and case studies. Just as important, numerous dissertations have come from the New DEEL perspective. The findings of their research are of interest to both scholars of educational leadership and practitioners. Many of these endeavors had their start at traditional academic conferences such as the American Educational Research Association (AERA), the University Council for Educational Administration (UCEA), the British Educational Leadership Management and Administration Society (BELMAS), and the National Council of Professors of Educational Administration (NCPEA). Others have begun as presentations at one of the six New DEEL conferences we have held at Temple University. This also links public intellectual work with ongoing participation in learned societies.

Combining public intellectual work with scholarship like this has been my focus for the past several years in articles, book chapters, and books. Perhaps the best example is *Ethical Educational Leadership in Turbulent Times: (Re)solving Moral Dilemmas*, which Joan Shapiro and I wrote and is now in its second edition. The book uses Multiple Ethical Paradigm, a theoretical construct that Joan and Jacqueline Stefkovich built, in combination with Turbulence Theory, which I have developed. With these two approaches, students from Joan's ethics course provide authentic ethical dilemmas and raise critical questions that push readers beyond superficial responses.

That is a key to our pursuit of a new kind of leader, since it transcends the simplistic notion of heroic leadership at one extreme and compliant leadership at the other. We insist that effective leadership for today's schools and universities needs to be much more sophisticated. We have developed a New DEEL vision for leaders outlined in the table below (Gross, 2009) to better describe the qualities we believe leaders at all levels need. The table below shows the transformational behaviors that New DEEL leaders have in contrast to the transactional behaviors exhibited by more traditional leaders:

Table 11.1. New DEEL Vision for Leaders.

New DEEL Vision for Leaders	Behavior of Traditional School Leaders
1. Guided by inner sense of responsibility to students, families, the community, and social development on a global scale.	Driven by an exterior pressure of accountability to those above in the organizational/political hierarchy.
2. Leads from an expansive community-building perspective. A democratic actor who understands when and how to shield the school from turbulence and when and how to use turbulence to facilitate change.	Bound by the system and the physical building. A small part of a monolithic, more corporate structure.
3. Integrates the concepts of democracy, social justice, and school reform through scholarship, dialogue, and action.	Separates democracy and social justice from guiding vision and accepts school improvement (a subset of school reform) as the dominant perspective.

4. Operates from a deep understanding of ethical decision making in the context of a dynamic, inclusive, democratic vision.	Operates largely from perspective of the ethic of justice wherein obedience to authority and current regulations is largely unquestioned, despite one's own misgivings.
5. Sees one's career as a calling and has a well-developed sense of mission toward democratic social improvement that cuts across political, national, class, gender, racial, ethnic, and religious boundaries.	Sees one's career in terms of specific job titles with an aim to move to ever-greater positions of perceived power within the current system's structure.

Clearly, we are asking a great deal of our students and ourselves as we try to model the behaviors we seek to instill in them. Each of the five New DEEL visions for leaders requires moving beyond traditional boundaries in order to guide schools in turbulent and ethically challenging times. For instance, narrow accountability pursued by the transactional leaders is replaced by a much more demanding standard of internal responsibility. But this can only be achieved through a continuing dialogue with students, parents, and community members. In this way, the New DEEL is inherently a public intellectual project.

I am currently co-authoring a book with Joan Shapiro that highlights the work of exemplars for each of these five areas when they faced a critical incident. The idea is to give readers authentic cases from which to draw inspiration and direction when they face the inevitable dilemmas inherent in our work. This is another example of public intellectual work combined with traditional scholarship. We are responding to significant questions in our field while simultaneously meeting the needs of practitioners and the communities they serve. Once completed, we expect to speak about this work at scholarly conferences as well as at public forums. Joan and I believe that these reinforce one another. However, not everyone agrees with us, and this has not been an easy road to travel. I will conclude this chapter with some lessons I have learned and some I am still trying to learn, rather late in the journey.

CONCLUSION

In a way, being a public intellectual is something of a paradox because it is both a privilege and a responsibility. It is a privilege to be able to speak on serious social issues to a wider audience with a degree of safety. For those of us who enjoy such a condition, I believe there is a responsibility to speak out. Otherwise, our freedom is wasted. So we are at once blessed with the freedom to act as public intellectuals while simultaneously obliged to take on that responsibility.

This paradox has caused me to think deeply about my own actions as a public intellectual. First, I believe that we should be conscious of the rarity of our situation and use this role with a balance of courage and care. For example, this means carefully preparing my remarks before groups like the Vermont State Board of Education, rehearsing my statements, and sharing my ideas respectfully. This allows me to use my strongest ideas, often highly critical of state policy, in a way that is heard. This practice is also in keeping with the fact that as a faculty member I represent my institution and my field.

Second, I try to be a considerate listener. In my opinion this is at least as important as speaking out. As a public intellectual I am trying hard to learn. To that end, listening with my full mind and heart is an indispensable habit. Listening also means creating dialogue and building community through respect. As someone who enjoys speaking in public, I will admit that quieting myself and learning to listen carefully is a challenge.

Third, I am trying to push the boundaries of my public intellectual work, and this has taken some interesting turns. Formal talks turn out to be the easiest for me. After all, I get introduced as a university professor, I have a topic, and there is an audience that, in theory, wants to hear what I have to share. Much more challenging are those occasions when I have to insert myself into an informal conversation, such as when I stop by Carol's Hungry Mind café back home in Middlebury, Vermont. I might be sitting with friends when someone raises the topic of education. That's when I join in, but it's hard because I could easily be overbearing and shut down the whole discussion. The habits of respect and listening help, but I am still learning how to do this kind of public intellectual work well.

These informal conversations matter because it is at these times, I believe, that people form their opinions on education issues and where we could have our greatest influence. But in order to take advantage of this opportunity, we have to change the dynamic. Think of it this way: if we were discussing an issue of medicine and a physician was in the room, we would expect a professional opinion from her. If we were discussing a matter of law and an attorney was with us, we would likewise expect a professional opinion from him. Yet when we discuss education issues, everyone acts as though they are the experts, likely because everyone has spent time in school. This is a missed opportunity for us, not to dominate the discussion, but to be who we are: thoughtful professionals bringing important facts to the dialogue. I don't think we are very good at this, yet I believe it is important for us to learn this new skill. It is critical public intellectual work.

Returning to our responsibilities, I believe that we have little choice but to act as public intellectuals with all of the strength we can muster. Otherwise we will continue to surrender our field to high-stakes accountability policies matched with dubious privatization schemes that harm children and cast a shadow on our public school system. Further, I believe that we can conduct our public intellectual practice in such a way that it bolsters rather than detracts from our academic work. When challenged, I respond that these experiences inform my scholarship and give me added credibility with my graduate students. We must also engage in serious discussions with our faculty colleagues and administrators at critical meetings, especially when we are asked to help revise procedures such as promotion and tenure.

While I can't meet with that class at Trinity College of Vermont again, I do speak with all of my current students about being public intellectuals. I ask them to see their classroom teaching or leadership building as integrally tied to the lives of people in the wider world. I try my best to model the behavior and the perspective I would like to see in them. It is liberating to cast off the old either-or dichotomy by accepting the idea that we are voices in a dynamic new chorus. We have the privilege and responsibility to act inside *and* beyond the academy. Perhaps our generation can strike just such a harmonious chord.

REFERENCES

Aronowitz, S., & Giroux, H.A. (1991). *Postmodern education: Politics, culture and social criticism.* Minneapolis: University of Minnesota Press.

Gross, S.J. (2009). (Re-)constructing a movement for social justice in our profession. In A.H. Normore (Ed.), *Leadership for social justice: Promoting equity and excellence through inquiry and reflective practice* (pp. 257–266). Charlotte, NC: Information Age Publishing.

Gross, S.J., & Shapiro, J.P. (2005, Fall). Our new era requires a new deel: Towards democratic ethical educational leadership. *UCEA Review*, pp. 1–4.

Koopman, O., Miel, A., & Misner, P. (1943). *Democracy in school administration.* New York: Appleton-Century.

Implications

CHAPTER TWELVE

Reimagining the Public Intellectual in Education

Making Scholarship Matter

CYNTHIA REYES AND CYNTHIA GERSTL-PEPIN

INTRODUCTION

We began this book project because we both were concerned about the lack of connection between academic research in education and the public's understanding of the challenges facing education. We had many conversations about the lack of alignment between our deep knowledge of education in connection to research we had conducted and the many challenges facing our culture in terms of poverty, racism, sexism, and homophobia. For us, the concern centers on the overly simplistic way these educational issues have been represented and misrepresented in the news media and public policy arenas. Both of us have sought to work as public scholars in macro arenas through radio guest appearances, legislative testimony and briefs, policy advocacy at the national level, and engaging the news media outlets, as well as micro arenas such as local district policy committees. Our engagement in these areas highlighted for us the political nature of the field of education research and the critical need for educational researchers to make connections between the academic world in which we worked and taught and the communities in which we lived. We yearned to capture the stories of other public scholars who struggled with how to make their research meaningful beyond academic arenas.

Through the course of this project we learned many things from our contributors in terms of the limitations and challenges of working as a public scholar and its critical importance for future generations of children. In this chapter, we want to highlight how the contributors to this book challenge education scholars to continue this work as well as point to the need for educational researchers to be more strategic in making their research useful and understandable to the public.

WHAT QUALIFIES AS RESEARCH? THROUGH THE LENS OF MINORITY VOICES

One of our greatest challenges in putting together this book was recruiting authors from historically marginalized groups. There has been a noticeable paucity of minority public intellectuals—in particular, women and individuals of color. The history of public intellectualism has attributed inspired thinking to such celebrated names as Antonio Gramsci (1971), Pierre Bourdieu (1980/1993), and Michel Foucault (1963/1994), most of whom were European males. Despite a critical presence of female public intellectuals such as Simone de Beauvoir, Susan Sontag, and even Black feminists such as bell hooks and Alice Walker, there still exists a strong association of the term "public intellectual" with being male (Oslender, 2007). In the social science field of education, women have played a significant role in the history of higher education, and yet more of them need to be recognized for their contribution to public thinking on education.

Over the years, there have been a number of women and minorities in the field who have contributed to public dialogues, including Maxine Greene (2000), Patti Lather (1991), Nel Noddings (1984), Diane Ravitch (2010), and Cornel West (2001). The idealized notion of a public intellectual, however, has typically not reflected the voices of women and minorities. In her germinal book *Decolonizing Methodologies* (1999), Maori scholar Linda Tuhiwai Smith wrote about how she chose to view research from the vantage point of one who had inherited a colonial history. She stated that "the term 'research,' is probably one of the dirtiest words in the indigenous world's vocabulary" (1999, p. 1). Smith deconstructs what it's like to work as both an insider in one's community and an outsider in the academy, and her writing offers a framework for those who desire to reclaim knowledge and research from an indigenous point of view. Although first published in 1999, her book and subsequent writings and activism on behalf of her Maori graduate students provide a beacon for myriad scholars from the Maori, Hawaiian, and Native American Indian communities.

A number of Internet blogs have even co-opted Dr. Smith's words (see, for example, Mia, 2011). These bloggers argue that Dr. Smith's work should not be seen as an outsider's view of conducting research in higher education, but as a much-needed response to the shifting of faces once perceived as the minority to the majority in a vastly changing global world. Smith wrote that scientific research was still predominantly westernized in its orientation. She questioned the ideology and the academic training that these ideals represented. With the exception of progress in feminist research and representation from women and some scholars of color (i.e., Cornel West and Robert Warrior), the status quo in what counts as research and how it is interpreted is still largely White and westernized. For those of us who teach and write in higher education, the global world outside has quickly become the global world inside, as both instructor and student wrestle with national issues that impact what we teach in the classroom. As a result, this book walks carefully but more urgently a fine line between serving an intellectual and a public audience.

The call for a diversity of voices is urgent, given the quickly changing demographics of our nation. The U.S. Census Bureau estimates that by 2042, Americans who identify themselves as Hispanic, Black, Asian, American Indian, Native American, and Pacific Islander will collectively outnumber non-Hispanic Whites (U.S. Bureau of the Census, 2008). More recently, the Census Bureau declared that White births no longer constitute a majority in the United States. Non-Hispanic Whites account for 49.6% of all births and represent a minority for the first time in our country's history, suggesting an emerging generational divide between a diverse young population and an older White one (Tavernise, 2012). Such a contrast raises important policy questions related to educating minority youth and the moral responsibility of older Americans to fiscally support the education of the younger, minority generation. The consequences of not educating the future generation or addressing the achievement gap among minority groups would be catastrophic to the future of our nation. The contributors to this book collectively raise the question of how educational scholars will help to steer a national conversation toward promoting research and policies concerning a minority group that has historically struggled to gain educational access. When is it the ethical responsibility of academic scholars, who are best able to understand the complexity of educational reform, to break down abstract theory and numbers and to communicate in the most accessible way to the general public? More important, how can research positively impact the very population it professes to serve when it is untranslatable and irrelevant because of the academic language?

While polarizing rhetoric does little to assuage the national discussion on race and poverty, the more inspirational and healing words of such Black female activists as bell hooks, Marion Edelman Wright, Patricia Hill Collins, and Audre Lorde do more to bridge differences. Ironically, the works of most scholars of color are not widely read across the university but are relegated to women's studies programs, sociology, educational philosophy and anthropology, or to qualitative research methodology courses. Lorde's essay "The Master's Tools Will Never Dismantle the Master's House" is important to consider here. She proposes to challenge patriarchy by seeking to engage it rather than submit to it. "Difference must be not merely tolerated, but seen as a fund of necessary polarities between which our creativity can spark like a dialectic" (2007, p. 467). Lorde's writing respects the role of disagreement and seeks to examine those very places where all women—the audience to whom this essay was addressed—can unite. In *Feminist Theory: From Margin to Center*, bell hooks grappled with the idea of using accessible literacy to teach all women—educated and uneducated—about feminism. She wrote that difficulty of access has always been a problem for communicating the ideas of feminist theory, and whether or not the "intellectual and scholarly pursuits were relevant to women as a collective group, to women in the 'real' world" (hooks, 2000, p. 110). The use of academic style made it impossible for educators to teach individuals who were not familiar with the style. She also wrote about the fear that many university professors had that their work would not be valued by other academics if they made it more accessible to a wider audience. She proposed that educators should also extend the mode of literacy from writing to dialogue so that women would be able to deconstruct through verbal communication the myths and stereotypes of feminism held by the general public. A seemingly radical departure from presenting theory, the writings of hooks, Lorde, and other scholars of color point to the reality that this is already happening, and that in some examples, theory and research is exploited and exaggerated to the general public. Their aim is to maintain the rigor and value of well-devised, theoretical work but also to consider matters of style in order to promote relevant and critical educational matters.

In taking up the need to consider how to communicate the most important education research of the day, we divided the book into three themes that reflected the issues that our contributing authors grappled with: making language accessible, engaging the public through news media, and personal dilemmas. These three sections explored the dimensions of a public intellectual from a variety of perspectives, extending the conversation on public scholarship and engaging different notions about what it means to be a public scholar in today's world.

MAKING ACADEMIC LANGUAGE ACCESSIBLE

The first section of the book, "Making Academic Language Accessible," raises the question of what accessibility should look like with regard to our responsibility as public scholars to share our research data with the public. The chapters in this section highlight two different ways in which one can view accessibility with educational research. In Chapter 1, "Crisscrossing from Classrooms to Cartoons: Social Science Satire," Michael Giangreco describes how he developed cartoons primarily to humanize the landscape of special disabilities. Robert Nash in Chapter 4, "Scholarly Personal Narrative as a Way to Connect the Academy to the World," emphasizes author voice and storytelling as a methodological responsibility for writing about research. Both chapters regard accessibility through the lens of written discourse or medium. Accessibility to academic language can be understood through the writing and medium one uses to communicate research data. In order for the public to find relevance in educational research, the public scholar must use something other than conventional, objective writing.

Giangreco's chapter raises the question of whether we (researchers) should become more immersed in—rather than distanced from—exploring different methods for engaging the actual and real experiences of students and teachers in the school. After having published prolifically on special disabilities and education, Giangreco began to translate some of his research findings and related issues about special education into cartoons that dramatically caught the attention of actual professionals, practitioners, and policymakers who worked in the field. Through cartoons, Giangreco felt more comfortable making commentary on some of the more absurd, as well as serious, standard professional practices that compelled him to publicly challenge the status quo in his field. He writes: "Discrimination against people with disabilities continues to be cloaked in the guise of benevolence, and too many pieces of the teaching, learning, and service delivery puzzle in schools do not logically fit together." Cartoons provided him an outlet to communicate these ideas, which engaged more debate as well as gave authentic language (besides academic and formal discourse) to more professionals who worked in the field.

For many years Nash has been writing about bridging the gap between scholars, students, and the general public. In his chapter he offers Scholarly Personal Narrative (SPN) as a style of public-intellectual writing grounded in "storytelling and self-disclosure, one that draws from a variety of academic and non-academic references and findings." In quoting Behar, Nash creates the methodology of the scholarly personal narrative to highlight the "self" in research and academic writing. His piece highlights the need to limit the "'depersonalizing trend' in research that results in massive collections of so-called 'objective data' regarding the 'other,' but nothing at all about the 'self' who is collecting the data." Modeling for his university students, Nash shared his own writing and engaged the students to share with each other so that meaning and knowledge were socially constructed and did not reside solely with the teacher. This method contrasts sharply with the limitations and requirements of gaining tenure in higher education, which Nash argues is no longer a draw and suggests reader-response feedback as a way to rejuvenate one's career in research writing.

Accessibility to research could also be viewed from a variety of semantic standpoints—namely, a power differential so common in the academy with regard to naming research and methodologies. For example, the term *public intellectual* presupposes a certain image and set of values for some of our contributors. In Chapter 2, "'Languaging Their Lives,' Places of Engagement, and Collaborations with Urban Youth," Valerie Kinloch creates new terminology in her writing/

research, the *languaging* of youth voices, because there exists no term within the field that conveys the interactions among youth, agency, and language in the public sphere. In Chapter 3, "Reframing: We Are Not Public Intellectuals; We Are Movement Intellectuals," Margarita Machado-Casas, Belinda Flores, and Enrique G. Murillo, Jr., invoke a more transformational view of the public intellectual and propose the term "movement intellectual" to redefine public scholarship as a form of agency.

The young men in Kinloch's study engaged in transformative work with each other to create cultural space in the public discussions of gentrification that occurred in their urban neighborhood. Kinloch reports that "they were struggling 'for the transformation for their places' by languaging their lives into ongoing, 'public' conversations (that they were not invited into), about a community that, for Khaleeq [one of the young men in the study], represents 'a new type of different that don't look like us.'" Kinloch asks the reader to be focused and mindful of what young people say as they share in the collective work of developing action with any civic-minded project. She says: "In this way we are doing the work of a public intellectual, or a public scholar, because the young people we collaborate with are teaching us how to do the work and why the work is so important." Kinloch's use of reflective poems also evokes the voices of her participants, Phillip and Khaleeq, as they share their vision for places of engagement. For Kinloch, it is critical not only to describe and interpret the experiences of the youth in her research, but also to have their voices be present in the transcripts of her dialogues with them (dialoging and languaging) and in the poetic devices that she uses to make the more fundamental point about doing this research: that "this narrative of engagement, collaboration, and change does not often get assigned to Black male youth in urban schools and communities."

Machado-Casas, Flores, and Murillo, Jr., confront the term "public intellectual" directly, suggesting that it is a subtractive concept mired in middle-class, Western values, and propose the term "movement intellectual" as an alternative. Their conceptualization of movement intellectual is based on their "*compromiso y necesidad de ver cambio* (commitment and the necessity to see change)" for linguistically and culturally diverse youth and their communities. Their shared desire creates something akin to what some Latino researchers in literacy education refer to as *third space* for engaging, negotiating with, and co-constructing scholarship that values the diversity of "socio-historical lives" (Gutierrez, 2008, p. 149). They argue that the term "movement intellectual" more accurately describes their work as part of a larger group of scholars working together as a force that is fluid, mobile, and proactive: a term based on an additive model that values a multitude of cultural experiences. By reframing their work as movement intellectuals, they broaden the concept of a public scholar to encompass scholars who see themselves as advocates for their communities.

In this section, the authors offer examples of how language in all its genres—from narrative, to poetic device, to graphic cartoon—could shape important policy conversations related to the field of education and widen the audience possibilities beyond the academic market. While the authors do not suggest that one replace the other, they question the dissemination of such research as being confined to an insular community and published in only a few higher education outlets. In response to this insularity, some of our contributors choose to re-appropriate the term "public intellectual" itself to more accurately describe the community engagement that is part of their work, and the ways in which researchers see their participants and see the work that they engage in with their participants. The next section critically considers how to share educational research through non-academic venues.

ENGAGING THE NEWS MEDIA AND WEB 2.0

Gone are the days that print newspapers and television news shows were the primary arena through which information about educational policy and reform issues were shared with the public. The authors in this section have been very intentional about thinking about how education issues are framed and presented through the news media, public discussions about education, and alternative Internet outlets. Their work suggests that public figures without much training in research or background in education often influence how educational issues are portrayed and represented in these public arenas. The chapters by Ohanian, Dorn, and Mathis in this section argue that there is a need for educational researchers to think carefully about what their research means for public debates and to consider taking a more active role in public discussions around education issues.

Chapter 5, "When a Public Intellectual Speaks Out But No One Hears Her, Does She Exist?" by Susan Ohanian, is a wake-up call to educational researchers in which the author argues that it is critically important that we pay attention to how educational policy issues are framed in public arenas—that we engage in the public life around us. Her experiences in graduate school and as a public advocate on behalf of teachers points to the need for us to think deeply about how we share our work with local teachers and schools. In particular, her research on who gets cited in the press highlights the fact that many "experts" quoted in the press at the national level are actually not academic researchers with university ties but are instead often working for institutions with a bias toward charter schools or particular private institutions such as the conservative Hoover Institute or the Fordham Institute. Ohanian's work points to the need for educational researchers to turn their research eye to the media in particular and to think strategically about how to share research beyond academic journals and professional conferences. She asks us to give serious thought to how we make our voices heard and how we go about contributing to public debates and discussions.

In Chapter 6, "The Naked Seminar: Blogging as Public Education Outside the Classroom," Sherman Dorn provides one answer to Ohanian's query concerning how we make our voices heard when the media limits our opportunity for input. Dorn highlights how academics have taken to the "Internet streets" (so to speak) to share their research and insight directly with the public. YouTube videos, websites, social media, and blogs provide alternative avenues through which academics can share their research and speak publicly about issues. In particular, Dorn shares the impetus behind his creation of his own blog, which he calls a "naked seminar," emphasizing its similarity to a classroom space, where he could teach about how academic freedom was being portrayed negatively in media coverage.

Bill Mathis, in Chapter 7, "The Public Intellectual: The Changing Context; Implications for Attributes and Practices," provides very concrete strategies for how educational scholars can enter public debates and engage the public. For example, he has suggestions for writing op-ed pieces and blogging, as well as engaging avenues such as newspaper, radio, and television programs. Mathis suggests that public scholars need to be strategic in how they share their research, to communicate ideas clearly in lay terms, and to not take political attacks personally but instead maintain high standards of ethical behavior.

Ohanian, Dorn, and Mathis all suggest that there is a critical need for public scholars willing to engage the news media, Internet forums, and non-academic digital venues as outlets for their research expertise. This will be critically important in order to challenge research that presents itself as objective when it is really value-laden and skews toward particular political viewpoints. Technological modes of communication are opening up new venues for communicating research knowledge. But just as these new avenues of public engagement present opportunities, the next section suggests that they also present dilemmas for the public scholar.

PERSONAL DILEMMAS

The experiences and personal journeys regarding public intellectual work and the personal dilemmas related to doing this type of work are resonant in the writings of both seasoned and new scholars who contributed to the section. These chapters raise two fundamental questions: How should we (re)define the public intellectual in the context of this book? In light of the "movement intellectual" that Machado-Casas, Flores, and Murillo, Jr., described in the first section of the book, are there other dimensions of a public intellectual one ought to consider? If so, what should they look like? It was appropriate to begin this section with Ayer's chapter, as he critiques the term "public intellectual" as a type of work that could only be completed by an elite few and on a level that is exclusive rather than inclusive. By referring to himself as a "stunt intellectual," Ayers, a senior scholar, evokes the image of an individual who was called upon to do the authentic work and activism of a public scholar in public spaces. Ayers also draws upon his teaching and work with students to inform what it means to be a good teacher and therefore a good citizen and public scholar. According to Ayers, "the challenge involves, as well, an ethical stance and an implied moral contract."

Ayers argues that since all individuals have the capacity to critically reflect on their lives and on the world, "We all experience life, think, and learn—we are each and all of us, then, intellectuals." We may do better to explore the different dimensions and dilemmas of a public scholar. However, the authors in this section suggest that the degree to which one is able to practice this scholarly work depends on one's placement in the academy. They highlight research and writing that they have enjoyed doing, often viewing their university positions as distant from the public work that they want to accomplish, but they have engaged in work that they care about as they strive to also meet the demands of a tenure-track system.

In Chapter 9, "Traveling Down a Desire Line: Surviving Where Academia and Community Meet," JuliAnna Ávila uses the metaphor of the desire line, or a direct line between two points, to describe the "multi-directional work" that she engaged in to meet the tenure requirements of her position, as well as the desire to do good in the world and to engage in acts that serve a larger purpose in her surroundings. As a new scholar, Ávila made intentional choices between analysis, editing, and development of future projects, but this process was slow, indirect, and challenging. Her path deviated from that of the official academic as she kept in mind the element of agency, the determination to allow for oneself the "parameters of what constitutes valuable work" in the academy. For Ávila, what it meant to be a public scholar was to include her work with marginalized youth and minority communities on language and literacy.

In Chapter 10, "Conversations That Matter: Community-Based Practice in Support of the Public Good," Alan and Barri Tinkler, also new scholars, regard their service work in the community as a responsibility and a natural extension of their academic life in the university. While acknowledging the value that the academy places on faculty productivity in terms of the volume of publication, they also argue the importance of combining scholarship and action to benefit the communities with which they have worked. They evoke the work of Paulo Freire, which provides a guiding model for how to advance social justice, "ensuring that practices emerge to meet the changing needs of individuals and communities within a dynamic world." Their former work as Peace Corps volunteers in Papua New Guinea informed their ability to integrate civic-minded endeavors and service learning in their university work. Highlighting the various service-learning projects that they have engaged in—from matching university tutors with individual local students who were English language learners, to advancing their teacher preparation program goals through work in the community, to involvement with high school reform in area schools—the Tinklers seek to harmonize community engagement with teacher preparation. For them, the epitome of what it means to be a public scholar relates to the action and effort to effect change in one's milieu.

Chapter 11, "An Inevitable Dichotomy...*Really*? Harmonizing Public Intellectual Work *with* Academic Work," by Steven Jay Gross, describes perhaps most fluidly the multi-dimensions of a public scholar by sharing the choices he made throughout his career in attempting to balance his academic work with public scholarship. It is therefore appropriate to end with Gross's chapter, because he has always seen public intellectual work and academic work as mutually supportive of each other, arguing that there is indeed a harmonizing effect between the two. He has experienced the interconnection between the two in his own life as he began his professional career as a teacher and then later when he engaged in curriculum work with a state department of education. The only time he felt limited in his capacity to act as a public scholar was when he became a university faculty member later in life as an untenured associate professor. During the short period of time he was given to gain tenure, he suddenly had to begin to shift his writing toward academic journals and away from the practitioner journals in which he had already established a respectable publishing record. It was only after he gained tenure that he refocused his writing and research to more public venues.

The contributors in this section reflect a continuum of engagement with public scholarship brought on by the dilemmas they have faced in balancing this work with the requirements of their university positions. While each chapter reflects a different view of the work of the public intellectual, they all speak to a sense of moral obligation and a principled need for public scholars to engage public debates at both the micro and macro levels. The narratives of Kinloch, Marchado-Casas, Flores, and Murillo, Jr., Ávila, Tinkler and Tinkler, and Gross suggest that this work is challenging for an assistant professor, although not impossible.

LOOKING FORWARD: MAKING EDUCATIONAL RESEARCH MATTER IN A DIGITAL, GLOCAL AGE

Given that we are living in a global world of digital connectedness, public information has become increasingly digitized as the public engages in twenty-first-century modes of learning (Tapscott, 2008). This has opened up new digital arenas for public discourse. For example, the political campaign of Howard Dean ushered in the notion of Internet-based civic engagement, campaigning, and political organizing (Hindman, 2005). Gone are the days when the newspaper or nightly news was the primary avenue for public information about political issues (Gerstl-Pepin, 2007). The world in which the notion of the public intellectual was first coined was a world where print media (such as newspapers) and electronic media (such as radio, film, and television) reigned supreme. As Ohanian, Dorn, and Mathis note, our evolving digital age, Internet media, and Web 2.0 are creating potential new outlets for the public as well as scholars. Traditional methods of dissemination no longer dominate. Education scholars have known about this disconnect for some time and have struggled with how to share their research with decision makers at all levels (Nash, 2004).

In addition, the connection between globalization and the digital age has lessened the divide between the local and global—or glocal—influences on education. The field of education needs public scholars who can inform national and international policy debates as well as education debates at the local, community level. Both arenas need attention. As Brooks and Normore (2009) note, "many educators now acknowledge that issues related to globalization influence their local practice" (p. 53). Public scholars, then, may need to work at both global and local levels, as education can be seen as a glocal endeavor (Brooks & Normore, 2009).

Given these shifting contexts, the contributors to this book suggest that there is a critical need for education researchers to share their work so that the general public can make informed decisions about educational policy. As noted earlier, the tenure and promotion process in academia prizes refereed journal articles and academic publications. So how does one balance the requirements of one's chosen career with a desire to advocate for reasoned decision making and a balance of research perspectives? One digital example of this is the website *indymedia*, which has become a space for a collective of scholars to publish their work. "The possibilities of digital reproduction have increased the availability of information to an unlimited virtual audience (both in space and time), an imagined community, in an expanded new space" (Oslender, 2007). And it is more urgent than ever to explore how dissemination vehicles such as the Internet and social media can share rigorous research, given the glut of media information in these new digital spaces and the probability of misinformed reporting.

Education has become a media topic on which everyone from a parent to a community member to a policymaker can be an "expert" based on Internet "research" that one collects indiscriminately. While it is critical that citizens are well informed and can gain access to high-quality information, much information on the Internet is neither of high quality nor based on systematic research. The use of misinformation disguised as research can be devastating in school contexts where the need for reform is dire but is driven by special interest groups who may be strictly self-serving. The call for educational scholars is one of great urgency, given the complexity of a media- and technology-rich society, and the individual chapters in this book evoke a moral dimension that includes courage and agency in order for one to be an effective public scholar.

What Does It Take to Be a Public Scholar in Today's World?

Ayers quotes from Said (1994) to evoke a profound view of the public scholar: "The role has an edge to it, for the intellectual must open spaces 'to raise embarrassing questions, to confront orthodoxy and dogma (rather than to produce them), to be someone who cannot easily be co-opted by governments or corporations, and whose *raison d'être* is to represent all those people and issues that are routinely forgotten or swept under the rug'" (p. 11). Ayers, Gross, and Ohanian go further to warn of the dangers of settling into apathy in the education field as a neoliberal climate pervades every corner of the educational landscape, where business models are increasingly used to run pre-K–16 education in our nation, and where the control of curriculum and teaching is increasingly taken out of teachers' hands and placed in the hands of a burgeoning pool of administrators in response to the argument that public education is broken. Ayers saw the current attack on public education "as an attack on democracy itself."

Scholars well recognized by the public, including Diane Ravitch, Henry Giroux, and Pedro Noguera, have taken on the response to this assault on public education. Yet the voices of those who commit to being public scholars in the world of education are as varied and diverse as the contributing authors to this book. Their stories reflect the day-to-day life of a university faculty member whose capacity to engage social justice is sometimes constrained by the responsibilities of teaching, advising, attending department meetings, doing research, and doing service. However, the one unifying element that ties these stories together is the ability to envision what public scholarship could look like even within the academy. Both Ayers and Gross argue for pressing on toward an education that is democratic and socially just, whether it means (1) developing an educational leadership program that teaches democracy and ethics working from the inside out, (2) collaborating with communities to co-construct a just method for teaching, (3) working with marginalized groups of students one at a time, or (4) continuing to use one's voice in public spaces to speak out. The present chapter has sought to describe a continuum in which the act of behaving like a public scholar could be reimagined across the various public spheres.

We would like to close with a quote from *The Wire* that we used in the preface, and which is a dialog between an academic researcher (Dr. Parenti) and a former police officer and teacher (Bunny). Bunny is frustrated with Parenti, who seems more concerned with his research than with the fact that the incredibly effective program for troubled youth they were both working on was being shut down.

Dr. David Parenti (academic): We get the grant, we study the problem, we propose solutions. If they listen, they listen. If they don't, it still makes for great research. What we publish on this is gonna get a lot of attention.

Howard "Bunny" Colvin (former police officer): From who?

Dr. David Parenti: From other researchers, academics.

Howard "Bunny" Colvin: Academics?! What, they gonn' study your study? [chuckles and shakes head] When do this shit change?

—*The Wire*, Season 4, Final Grades Episode (Simon & Johnson, 2006)
© [2006], Home Box Office, Inc. All Rights Reserved, used with permission

In closing, we would like to suggest that all educational researchers have the potential to address Bunny's concerns and work beyond the borders of academia, to care about what is in front of us—the communities in which we live, work, and conduct research. The narratives in this book highlight the potential and the need for this work and provide examples of public scholars engaged in this work. We hope this is only the beginning of an understanding of the potential role a public scholar can play at both the macro and micro levels so that, as Howard "Bunny" Colvin stated in language that only his constituencies from *The Wire* could understand, the "sh*t" can change.

REFERENCES

Bourdieu, P. (1993). How can "free-floating intellectuals" be set free? In *Sociology in question* (R. Nice, Trans., pp. 41–48). London: Sage. (Original work published 1980)

Brooks, J.S., & Normore, A.H. (2009). Educational leadership and globalization: Literacy for a glocal perspective. *Educational Policy, 24*(1), 52–82.

Foucault M. (1994). *The birth of the clinic*. New York: Vintage Books. (Original work published 1963)

Gerstl-Pepin, C.I. (2007). Introduction to the special issue on media, democracy, and the politics of education. *Peabody Journal of Education, 82*(1), 1–9.

Gramsci, A. (1971). *Selections from the prison notebooks of Antonio Gramsci*. New York: International Publishers.

Greene, M. (2000). *Releasing the imagination: Essays on education, the arts, and social change*. San Francisco, CA: Jossey-Bass.

Gutierrez, K. (2008). Developing a sociocritical literacy in the third space. *Reading Research Quarterly, 43*(2), 148–164.

Hindman, M. (2005). The real lessons from Howard Dean: Reflections on the first digital campaign. *Perspectives on Politics, 3*(1), 121–128.

hooks, b. (2000). *Feminist theory: From margin to center*. Cambridge, MA: South End Press.

Lather, P. (1991). *Getting smart: Feminist research and pedagogy within/in the postmodern*. New York: Routledge.

Lorde, A. (2007). *Sister outsider: Essays and speeches by Audre Lorde.* New York: Ten Speed Press.

Mia. (2011, September 30). Conceptualizing Tuscarora: Language, culture, and the academy. Blogging hesitation [Web blog post]. Retrieved at http://conceptualizingtuscarora.wordpress.com/2011/09/30/blogging-hesitation/

Nash, R.J. (2004). *Liberating scholarly writing: The power of personal narrative.* New York: Teachers College Press.

Noddings, N. (1984). *Caring.* Berkeley: University of California Press.

Oslender, U. (2007). The resurfacing of the public intellectual: Towards the proliferation of public spaces of critical intervention. *ACME: An International E-Journal for Critical Geographies,* 6(1), 98–123.

Ravitch, D. (2010). *The death and life of the great American school system: How testing and choice are undermining education.* New York: Basic Books.

Simon, D. (Writer), & Johnson, C. (Director). (2006). Final grades [Television series episode]. In D. Simon & E. Burns (Executive producers), *The wire.* New York: HBO Time Warner.

Smith, L.T. (1999). *Decolonizing methodologies: Research and indigenous peoples.* London: Zed Books.

Tapscott, D. (2008). *Growing up digital: How the net generation is changing your world.* New York: McGraw-Hill.

Tavernise, S. (2012, May 17). Whites account for under half of births in the US. *The New York Times.* Retrieved from http://www.nytimes.com/2012/05/17/

U.S. Bureau of the Census. (2008, August 14). *An older more diverse nation by midcentury.* Retrieved from http://www.census.gov/newsroom/releases/archives/population/cb08–123.html

West, C. (2001). *Race matters.* New York: Beacon Books.

Author Biographies

JuliAnna Ávila is an Assistant Professor at The University of North Carolina at Charlotte, where she teaches undergraduate and graduate courses in English Education and digital literacies. A former high school teacher, she received her Ph.D. from The University of California at Berkeley and has published in *English Journal, Teaching Education, Theory Into Practice, Pedagogies,* and *Teachers College Record.* With Jessica Zacher Pandya, she is the co-editor of *Critical Digital Literacies as Social Praxis: Intersections and Challenges* (Lang, 2012) and *Moving Critical Literacies Forward: A New Look at Praxis Across Contexts* (Routledge, 2013). Her current research focuses on the utilization of digital composing to explore critical literacies with pre- and in-service English teachers.

William Ayers, formerly Distinguished Professor of Education and Senior University Scholar at the University of Illinois at Chicago (UIC), founder of both the Small Schools Workshop and the Center for Youth and Society, has written extensively about social justice, democracy and education, the cultural contexts of schooling, and teaching as an essentially intellectual, ethical, and political enterprise. His articles have appeared in numerous scholarly and popular journals, and his books include *Teaching Toward Freedom; A Kind and Just Parent; Fugitive Days; On the Side of the Child; Teaching the Personal and the Political;* (with Ryan Alexander-Tanner) *To Teach: The Journey, in Comics;* (with Kevin Kumashiro, Erica Meiners, Therese Quinn, and David Stovall) *Teaching Toward Democracy;*

(with Bernardine Dohrn) *Race Course*. Edited books include (with Janet Miller) *A Light in Dark Times: Maxine Greene and the Unfinished Conversation*; (with Therese Quinn and Jean Ann Hunt) *Teaching for Social Justice*; and (with Therese Quinn and David Stovall) the *Handbook of Social Justice in Education*.

Sherman Dorn is the Director of the Division of Educational Leadership and Innovation at Arizona State University's Mary Lou Fulton Teachers College. His books trace how our society defines school problems and how those definitions shape education policy. In *Creating the Dropout* (1996), Dorn points out that dropping out became defined as a crisis in the 1960s when the proportion of teens graduating from high school had been rising for years. In *Accountability Frankenstein* (2007), he explains how we have come to distrust schoolteachers but trust test scores. In each case, he documents the inconsistencies in education policy and how popular thinking leads to unproductive education policy. He is editor of *Education Policy Analysis Archives*, one of the main peer-reviewed education policy journals in the United States and a pioneer in electronic publication. In addition to writing books on dropping out and accountability, Sherman Dorn is the coeditor of books on school communities and Florida education policy, the author of several articles and book chapters on the history of special education, several pieces on academic freedom in higher education, and writes an active blog entitled the *One Blog Schoolhouse*.

Belinda Bustos Flores, Professor, University of Texas at San Antonio, completed her Ph.D. at the University of Texas, Austin in Curriculum and Instruction with specializations in Multilingual Studies and Educational Psychology. In 2000, she received the 1st place award for Outstanding Dissertation from The National Association for Bilingual Education (NABE). She was awarded the 2004 UTSA President's Distinguished Award for Research Excellence. Her research interests and publications in peer reviewed, Tier I journals focus on teacher development including self-concept, ethnic identity, efficacy, beliefs, teacher recruitment/retention, and high stakes testing. Publications also focus on teacher sociocultural knowledge of family cultural literacy. Dr. Flores' work has been cited in top journals such as the *BRJ, Curriculum Inquiry, Curriculum Studies, Educational Researcher, Educational Administration Quarterly, Educational Studies, Handbook of Teacher Education, Journal of Early Childhood Teacher Education, Journal of Latinos & Education, Journal of Hispanic Higher Education, Multicultural Perspectives, Teachers College Record, The Reading Teacher, The Urban Review*, and *Young Children*. An upcoming Routledge edited book, *Preparing Teachers for Bilingual Student Populations: Educar para Transforma* (Flores, Sheets, Clark, 2011) is expected to transform the preparation of teachers and teacher educators alike.

Cynthia Gerstl-Pepin is an Associate Dean and Professor for the College of Education and Social Services at the University of Vermont. Dr. Gerstl-Pepin is an interdisciplinary scholar who explores the social justice implications concerning how poverty and other forms of discrimination may have an impact on education inequity. As a policy scholar and qualitative methodologist she is specifically interested in the frequent disconnect between public policies and their portrayals in the media and the lived realities of the children, teachers, staff, and administrators who inhabit schools and the communities they serve. Dr. Gerstl-Pepin served as a Fulbright Scholar in 2010 at Beijing Normal University in the People's Republic of China. Her teaching interests center on the politics of education, qualitative methodology, and diversity issues. She is the co-author of *Reframing Educational Politics for Social Justice* (with Catherine Marshall), and she has been published in such journals as the *Journal of School Leadership*, *Educational Policy*, *Teachers College Record*, *International Journal of Qualitative Studies in Education*, *Qualitative Research*, and *Review of Higher Education*.

Michael F. Giangreco, Ph.D., is a Professor in the Department of Education (Special Education Program) at the University of Vermont and is also affiliated with the Center on Disability & Community Inclusion. Prior to joining the faculty at UVM in 1988 he served in a variety of capacities (e.g., community residence counselor with adults with disabilities, special education teacher, special education administrator). His work focuses on various aspects of education for students with disabilities within general education classrooms such as curriculum planning and adaptation, related services decision-making and coordination, alternatives to over reliance on paraprofessionals and inclusive special education service delivery. Dr. Giangreco is the author of numerous professional publications on a variety of special education topics and has published a series of cartoons depicting educational issues and research findings.

Steven Jay Gross is Professor of Educational Administration at Temple University. Gross's teaching, books, articles, and research activities focus on initiating and sustaining democratic reform in schools and Turbulence Theory. His books include: *The Handbook on Ethical Educational Leadership* (2014) (co-edited with Christopher Branson), *Ethical Educational Leadership in Turbulent Times* (2008,2013)(co-authored with Joan P. Shapiro), *Leadership Mentoring* (2006), *Staying Centered: Curriculum Leadership in a Turbulent Era* (1998), and *Promises Kept: Sustaining School and District Leadership in a Turbulent Era* (2004). Gross served as Editor of ASCD's *Curriculum Handbook* series and as a Senior Fellow at the Vermont Society for the Study of Education. Gross was also Chief of Curriculum and Instruction for the State of Vermont, Associate Professor of Education at Trinity College of Vermont, and Curriculum and Staff Development Director for the Rutland Northeast Supervisory

Union in Vermont, and a high school social studies teacher in Philadelphia. Gross is a leading figure in a movement called the New DEEL (Democratic-Ethical Educational Leadership) and serves as the Founding Director of the New DEEL Community Network at Temple University. The New DEEL promotes the values of democracy, social justice, and authentic learning in schools and includes colleagues from over thirty universities as well as numerous school districts in the U.S., Canada, U.K., Hong Kong, Sweden, Australia, New Zealand, Taiwan, and Jamaica. Gross has been Distinguished Visiting Research Scholar (Australian Catholic University) and is on the roster of the Fulbright Specialist Program.

Valerie Kinloch is Professor of Literacy Studies in the Department of Teaching and Learning and Director of the Office of Diversity of Inclusion in the College of Education and Human Ecology at The Ohio State University. She holds affiliate appointments in the Department of English and the Department of Women's Studies at OSU. Her research interests focus on the social and literary lives and collaborative engagements of youth and adults in and out-of-school spaces, particularly in urban contexts. She is the author of several journal articles, including "Revisiting the Promise of Students' Right to Their Own Language: Pedagogical Strategies" (in *College Composition and Communication Journal*), "'The White-ificaton of the Hood': Power, Politics, and Youth Performing Narratives of Community" (in *Language Arts Journal*), "'To Not Be a Traitor of Black English': Youth Perceptions of Language Rights in an Urban Context," in *Teachers College Record*), and, among other articles, "Suspicious Spatial Distinctions: Literacy Research with Students Across School and Community Contexts" (in *Written Communication*). Her co-authored book, *Still Seeking an Attitude: Critical Reflections on the Work of June Jordan*, was released in 2004, and her single-authored biography on poet-educator June Jordan titled *June Jordan: Her Life and Letters* was published in 2006. Dr. Kinloch was awarded a Spencer Foundation Small Research Grant as well as a Grant-in-Aid from the National Council of Teachers of English (NCTE) to support her work on the writing, literacy, and activist practices of African American and Latino/a high school and first generation college students in urban settings. In particular, this work examines how community gentrification and a politics of place can heavily impact the lives, literacy practices, and survival strategies of urban youth of color. Her book, *Harlem on Our Minds: Place, Race, and the Literacies of Urban Youth*, won the 2012 Outstanding Book of the Year Award from the American Educational Research Association (AERA).

Margarita Machado-Casas is an Associate Professor at The University of Texas at San Antonio in the College of Education and Human Development, Division of Bicultural-Bilingual Studies. Dr. Machado-Casas completed her Ph.D. at University of North Carolina at Chapel Hill, and was awarded the IMPACT award for her research on transnational migration trends of newly arrived immigrants in the U.S. South and its effects in Education. Dr. Machado-Casas also completed a prestigious post-doctoral fellowship at Frank Potter Graham (FPG) Research Institute at UNC-Chapel Hill.

Her research interests include migrant, Afro-descendents, indigenous and Latino education, transnational communities, and minority agency in the fields of education, assessment/evaluation, parent/family involvement, and social cultural foundations. She has provided leadership development sessions both nationally and internationally, as well as language, literacy, assessment/evaluation, and cultural diversity training to area school districts. Dr. Machado-Casas is an Education Consultant and has taught elementary school, graduate and undergraduate education courses. She is currently the Co-Chair for the Language Policy SIG for the National Association of Bilingual Educators (NABE). She is a board member of several prestigious academic journals and is currently a co-editor for the *Handbook of Latinos in Education*. She has worked with national and international governments and non-profit organizations.

William J. Mathis is the Managing Director of the National Education Policy Center, University of Colorado at Boulder. He previously served as superintendent of schools for the Rutland Northeast Supervisory Union in Brandon, Vermont, and was a national superintendent of the year finalist as well as Vermont superintendent of the year. Earlier, he was Deputy Assistant Commissioner in New Jersey and worked with a number of colleges and universities on a full-time or adjunct basis. He has published and presented to a wide variety of professional and lay audiences on finance, assessment, accountability, school vouchers, cost-effectiveness, education reform, history, special education, and Constitutional issues. He serves as a member of the Vermont state board of education and on the national board of directors of the Rural School and Community Trust. He previously served on the board for the Association for Education Finance and Policy.

Enrique G. Murillo, Jr., Ph.D. is a Professor at California State University, San Bernardino and Executive Director of Latino Education & Advocacy Days (LEAD). He is a first generation Chicano, born and raised in the greater East side of Los Angeles, and a native bilingual speaker in Spanish/English. He has also conducted research in several community-based organizations organizing cultural celebrations for newly arrived Latino immigrants, dealing specifically with issues of identity, diversity, and socialization rituals in the planning and performances of these cultural festivals. He serves as the founding Editor for the *Journal of Latinos and Education* and has published numerous articles in various academic journals including *Educational Foundations*, *The Urban Review*, *Journal of Thought*, *Educational Studies*, *Anthropology and Education Quarterly*, and *International*

Journal of Qualitative Studies in Education. He is co-author/co-editor of several books, *Local Democracy Under Siege* with NYU Press; *The New Latino Diaspora* with Ablex Press; *Post-Critical Ethnography in Education* with Hampton Press; and the *Handbook of Latinos and Education* with Routledge.

Robert J. Nash has been a Professor in the College of Education and Social Services, University of Vermont, Burlington, for 41 years. He specializes in philosophy of education, applied ethics, higher education, and religion, spirituality, and education. He holds graduate degrees in English, Theology/Religious Studies, Applied Ethics and Liberal Studies, and Educational Philosophy. He has published more than 100 articles in many of the leading journals in education at all levels. He has also published several book chapters, monographs, and essay book reviews. He is a member of the editorial board for the *Journal of Religion & Education,* and is one of its frequent contributors. Since 1996, he has published ten books (all still in print), several of them national award winners: *"Real World" Ethics: Frameworks for Educators and Human Service Professionals* (1st edition); *"Real World" Ethics: Frameworks for Educators and Human Service Professionals* (2nd edition); *Answering the "Virtuecrats": A Moral Conversation on Character Education; Faith, Hype, and Clarity: Teaching About Religion in American Schools and Colleges; Religious Pluralism in the Academy: Opening the Dialogue; Spirituality, Ethics, Religion, and Teaching: A Professor's Journey; Liberating Scholarly Writing: The Power of Personal Narrative; How to Talk About Hot Topics on Campus: From Polarization to Moral Conversation,* first author with DeMethra L. Bradley and Arthur W. Chickering. *Teaching Adolescents Religious Literacy in a Post-9/11 World,* first author with Penny Bishop; *Helping College Students Find Purpose: The Campus Guide to Meaning-Making,* first author with Michele Murray.

Currently a freelance writer, **Susan Ohanian's** writing draws on her own long career as a teacher grades K–14 and on current corporate-politico assaults on public education. Her more than 300 essays on education issues have appeared in periodicals ranging from Phi Delta Kappan cover stories to commentary in such fare as *The Nation, Washington Monthly, The Atlantic,* and *USA Today.* Three recent titles of Susan's 25 books reveal her interest in both the politics of schooling and the importance of curriculum—and her insistence that it all must come back to children: *When Childhood Collides with NCLB, Why Is Corporate America Bashing Our Public Schools?* and *The Whole Word Catalogue: FUNdamental Activities for Building Vocabulary.* Susan's website of resistance to high stakes testing and No Child Left Behind received the George Orwell Award for Distinguished Contributions to Honesty and Clarity in Public Language from the National Council of Teachers of English. She is also a recent recipient of the Kenneth S. Goodman "In Defense of Good Teaching" Award, College of Education, University of Arizona.

Cynthia Reyes is an Associate Professor of middle level education in the College of Education and Social Services at the University of Vermont. Her research interests include a social and cultural approach to literacy practice, digital literacy, identity and youth, race and language policy, and educational foundations. She is the author of book chapters and journal articles in *Research in the Teaching of English*, *The Reading Teacher*, *Educational Foundations*, *Journal of Public Affairs Education*, and *Teacher Education & Practice*. As a former middle grades bilingual classroom teacher in the Chicago Public Schools, she became engaged with issues of language acquisition, bilingual and bicultural identity, and immigration. She currently serves as the primary investigator for the Vermont Adolescent Literacy & Learning initiative of the Vermont Reads Institute, and she is the State Representative for the Northern New England TESOL. Her current work is focused on integrating practice and policy on working with English language learners in K-12.

Alan Tinkler, Ph.D., is an Assistant Professor in the Department of Education at the University of Vermont. He is a 2014 Lynton Award Finalist, an early career award for the scholarship of engagement. He works closely with various community centers, including King Street Center and the O'Brien Community Center in Vermont, to develop meaningful academic support and advocacy programming to empower community youth. He co-edited a book, *Transforming Teacher Education through Service-Learning*, which came out in 2013. He was a Peace Corps volunteer in Papua New Guinea and has a Ph.D. in English from the University of Denver.

Barri Tinkler, Ph.D., is an Assistant Professor in the Department of Education at the University of Vermont. She began her teaching career as a Peace Corps volunteer in Papua New Guinea and then taught eighth and ninth grade social studies in Stillwater, Oklahoma. Her research focuses on the impact of service-learning on preservice teachers' understanding of diversity. She is co-editing a book, *Service-Learning to Advance Social Justice in a Time of Radical Inequality*, which will come out in 2015. She has a Ph.D. in curriculum and instruction from the University of Denver.

Index

Studies in the Postmodern Theory of Education

General Editor
Shirley R. Steinberg

Counterpoints publishes the most compelling and imaginative books being written in education today. Grounded on the theoretical advances in criticalism, feminism, and postmodernism in the last two decades of the twentieth century, Counterpoints engages the meaning of these innovations in various forms of educational expression. Committed to the proposition that theoretical literature should be accessible to a variety of audiences, the series insists that its authors avoid esoteric and jargonistic languages that transform educational scholarship into an elite discourse for the initiated. Scholarly work matters only to the degree it affects consciousness and practice at multiple sites. Counterpoints' editorial policy is based on these principles and the ability of scholars to break new ground, to open new conversations, to go where educators have never gone before.

For additional information about this series or for the submission of manuscripts, please contact:

Shirley R. Steinberg
c/o Peter Lang Publishing, Inc.
29 Broadway, 18th floor
New York, New York 10006

To order other books in this series, please contact our Customer Service Department:

(800) 770-LANG (within the U.S.)
(212) 647-7706 (outside the U.S.)
(212) 647-7707 FAX

Or browse online by series:
www.peterlang.com